AF415921

WITHIN: A THREE PART HORROR

BOOK ONE OF THE WITHIN SERIES

EDMUND STONE

RIVER REVIVAL PRESS, LLC

Within: A Horror in Three Parts

Copyright © 2023 by Edmund Stone

All rights reserved.

No part of the book may be reproduced in any form or

by any electronic or mechanical means,

including information storage and retrieval systems,

without written permission from the author,

except the use of brief quotations in a book review.

Thai book is a work of fiction. Any references to

historical events, real people, or real places are used

fictitiously.

Other names, characters, places, and events are products

of the authors imagination,

and any semblance to actual events, or places or persons,

living or dead, is entirely coincidental.

Edited by Amber Applegate

Cover art by Maisie Stokely

Formatting by Edmund Stone

DEDICATION

To Mikel, my wife, my love, my reason for every day.
To my children and grandchildren,
McKenzie, Lauren, Parker,
Laynie, Carver, Ellie, and Beau,
Never stop dreaming.

To the readers and reviewers of this work.
Thank you one and all
For the contributions you made
To making this book
The best it could be.

EDMUND STONE

Trigger warning on last page

Within You Within

B ecca rocked her baby, as the house creaked from the onslaught of the wind outside, announcing the call of the storm to come. It gave her pause, even fear, as she was all alone with only her baby on her chest. She watched Toby suckle her breast, as he snuggled close to her, and she inhaled his newborn scent. The best smell she'd ever experienced in her life.

A thump hit the house. She jumped, startling Toby, causing him to detach from her and cry. "There, there," she said as she rocked him gently.

She let him latch back onto her, then stood and pulled the curtain back from the window to peek outside. The noise came from the front porch. The glider most likely. It banged again and she thought it a good idea to pull the thing away from the outside wall before it woke Toby again. Becca hated being alone, especially on a night like this. If Chad was here, he could take care of it, but not today. Her husband wouldn't be home until later tonight.

Her glasses fell forward on her nose, and she pushed them up with her free hand. They were an aggravation but one she had to deal with since she'd run out of her packs of contact lenses. She wished she didn't need them, but without them the world was a blur. Becca's robe gaped open, sending cold chills over her naked body. Earlier, she'd hurried from the shower when she heard Toby fussing, barely having the time to get her robe on, let alone tie the thing. Toby grabbed for her breast when she picked him up and she couldn't leave him to go put clothes on, so she had to make do with the robe. No one was around to see her but she was still self-conscious. The baby weight was stubborn to come off, tepidly responding to any of the exercises she did. She supposed she could be more diligent, but Toby took up so much of her time and she wanted the house to look nice when Chad was home. She thought being a stay home mom would be easy, but the opposite proved true. It was tough, much more than she realized, but every time she looked at Toby's innocent face, she knew it was worth it.

Becca could manage a little while longer until Chad came home. He should've been here already. It was Friday night and long-haul truckers came home on the weekend, at least the respectable ones like Chad. She could take care of herself, but it would be much easier if he were here.

The wind chime hanging on the porch sang loudly, as it twirled frantically from a fresh gust of wind. The haunting song it played suited the Fall night. Becca normally loved the sound, but tonight it seemed out of place. Like something from a horror movie. The ones Chad loved, and she loathed. Chad would stay up late watching them and she tried to ignore the noise, but the screams of terror and heightened music score made it difficult to sleep.

Becca shuddered as another chill crept over her body. She noticed everything was hitting the house on the east side, meaning the weather was coming the same way and Becca knew storms from that direction were the worst. Her daddy had a funny saying, *winds from the east, the fishing's the least, winds from the west, the fishing's the best.*

She grew up on the Atlantic coastline and her daddy taught her to look to the east for hurricanes. She never forgot it. Clyde Holston was a weather watcher to the core. He had a passion for it, as he always kept his weather radio on. Even when there was no storm brewing, erecting windsocks on the edge of their property to gage the direction of the storm. Libby, Becca's mommy, put up with his obsession, but seemed to always have a distaste for it, treating it as something not worthy of attention.

But her daddy proved himself every time a hurricane brewed. He went into action, covering all the windows with wood, bracing for the worst. Becca's family always rode out hurricanes in the underground shelter he had built. Those nights created vivid memories of huddling together with her daddy's wind up weather radio, listening to the beeps and squelches that haunted her to this day. The way it was loud at first, then began to fade and the crackle when her daddy brought it back to life again. She'd fall asleep in her mommy's arms, only to wake to the sound of creaking wood and bellowing wind. It burned a special terror in the recesses of her mind, and she relived it every time a storm came. The memory of Becca, her mommy, daddy, and Christopher, her twin brother, all huddled together in the storm shelter under their house left an indelible imprint on her psyche, especially the way her mommy felt about her brother.

Libby Holston hated Christopher. A fact Becca realized when her mommy would try and silence her brother, calling him an abomination. A word she had no reference for at the time but would understand fully as she got older. She supposed it was because Christopher always got her into trouble, but he meant no harm, he only liked to play. The only problem was he had little regard for authority and his playing pushed the boundaries of what mommy would allow. When Becca was with him, she felt the same, and got into trouble.

Libby never approved of Becca's relationship with her brother and tried to separate them all the time. It saddened Becca, because during those stressful times she leaned on him the most. Becca started to understand her mommy's feelings for Christopher came from Becca's dependence on him. It was evident during the storm when her mommy tried to take Christopher's place. But Becca wouldn't have it and pushed back to allow Christopher to stay with her. Libby conceded but wasn't happy about it. Becca remembered how he whispered to her during the storm, soothing her frayed nerves with his soft southern drawl.

"Hush now, the storm will pass, this is one of many to come. We'll get through them together. Take it easy and breathe," he'd say, calming her mind. Then he'd sing a song they both knew. One from the video tape with the purple dinosaur mommy played when she wanted to get work done around the house. Christopher sang in a sing-song melody, almost teasing, *"I love you, you love me, we're a happy family."*

He was such a child and never took anything seriously. Because of this, Christopher was the rock she leaned on when she needed a break from the real world. She'd probably still be with him if Chad Jeremy Riser hadn't come along. Chad was jealous of Christopher in his own way, but she didn't mind. Her husband helped her see she was more than what she was with her brother. With Chad she was an adult with adult responsibilities. Her brother lived in a child's world and probably always would.

Libby had Christopher locked away in some cold hospital, away from home, all because of her mommy's hatred toward him. Becca was admitted too but only because she loved Christopher so much and didn't want to be apart from him. When Becca left the institution, Christopher stayed behind, and Becca would never forgive any of them for taking her brother from her. Daddy supported her, urging her to come home, but not Libby. Becca's mommy would rather see her gone and she knew it.

Even though her mommy and Chad wanted him to stay there, she still longed for his calming words, especially while the wind blew outside. His whispers of reassurance the storm would pass. Although she kept an eye on the weather, some things, either good or bad, you never forgot. She wanted her brother's memory to be high in that category.

Becca opened the front door and stepped onto the porch, holding the now sleeping Toby against her chest. Immediately the wind whipped her hair around, and she turned her back to protect her baby as he slept against her chest.

The glider banged against the house, leaving a scrape on the white paint. She stepped to the metal chair and hooked a foot on the bottom. Then balancing on the other foot, pulled it away from the house. It continued to swing wildly but hadn't the reach to hit anything. A thumping sound, much lighter than the glider came from behind her. She turned to see their Bloodhound, Homer, beating a rhythm of happiness on the wood of the porch. He licked Becca's hand, then pushed against her while rubbing his head on her palm, seeking affection.

Becca sniffed the warm night air. It was maybe sixty or seventy degrees she figured; a feeling reminiscent of Summer. This season of fair temperatures seemed to hold on for some reason, but Becca enjoyed it. The longer the warm nights stayed around the better she handled things. Winter made it harder to endure the long nights missing her husband and the cold only added to the pain. A sense of desperation to bolt for something, Christopher if she could, came over her during the winter months. She lived two hours away from her family. If Chad continued his trucking job through those months, she'd seriously consider moving in with her mommy and daddy. She quickly removed the thought, realizing she couldn't go there, not with the way Libby treated poor Christopher, and her for that matter.

She thought about the days after she left the hospital and how grueling they were. Libby Holston was overbearing, never wanting Becca to go out of the house. Becca was old enough to know better, as she was seventeen by then. She was ready to move on, away from her controlling mom, even if the woman told her she was sick. Libby was the sick one, Becca realized, leaving her to rot in the hospital and trying to hide her issues. When Chad came along, Becca ran away with him and never looked back.

Toby moved against her, bringing her back to the present with his mouth rutting and wandering toward her breast. Pulling the milk engorged tit out of her robe—the state they were always in these days—she led him to it, and he sucked greedily. It hurt a little, as her breast were sore from this little veracious eater, but Becca didn't mind at all. Her motherhood was a thing of pride, and she relished the chance to feed her child. It empowered her to a point and helped her to forget about the bouts of sadness she experienced after he was born. Post partum depression is what the doctors called it and put Becca on medication for the condition. She hated the way it erased her libido and made her not care about anything. So, she stopped taking it shortly after it was prescribed. Something Chad didn't know about. If he did, he never would've left for work.

Becca wanted to feel good and laugh at the funny things Chad would say. Like the way he marveled at how good an eater his boy was, and how he was a chip off the old block the way he went after her tits. He'd taken a drink of her milk himself on occasion after Becca teased him with it, and they both laughed when he did. Afterward, when they went to bed, Chad held her close, pulling his body into hers, melting together. Thinking about those special times made Becca miss him even more.

Toby continued to suckle while Becca peered up the driveway, her hair blowing in her face. She tried to flip it back without disturbing the baby causing her glasses to fall to the middle of her nose again. She tried to get them back to position by flipping her head, but it didn't work. A glint of something near the end of the driveway caught her attention and Becca tried to concentrate on the area, squinting her eyes to focus as best she could.

Maybe it was Chad's rig? She thought. But why would he park there and not come into the house? Her robe lifted from the torrent of wind and the warm air invaded her midsection, waking up her senses to her nakedness underneath. She pushed it down, attempting to cover herself with her free hand as the wind lifted it again. She had no shoes on either and the small rocks in the unpaved drive were digging into her feet, but Becca ignored the pain and eased a few steps up the driveway, trying to get a better look at what was out there.

A pit rose in her stomach from the fear of the night and the approaching storm and Becca suddenly didn't want to be outside. Homer was by her side, he would keep any predators at bay, but even he was afraid of the storm. He whined, as the wind picked up causing Becca's hair and robe to become an unruly mess. Strands of hair fell between her glasses and her eyes, making it even harder to see. As she approached the item she saw from the porch, she realized the shining metal was no more than the mailbox glinting in the moon's light as it passed between the clouds. Homer went to investigate, sniffing the post of the mailbox, then hiking his leg and depositing a stream of urine. He then returned to her side and sat waiting for further instruction.

This was insane. Why was she standing out here? She decided to give Chad a call—what she should've done in the first place—to see if he was close. She shifted Toby's weight to one side to free up her hand and fished in the robe pocket for her phone but didn't find it. Of course, it wasn't there, because it was charging on the kitchen countertop, she remembered. Becca sighed and headed for the house.

The wind picked up and blew the flailing robe around her body again. She made a feeble attempt to hold it together, but it was no use. The terrycloth covering gaped open, displaying her naked body for the world to see. The closest neighbor was at least a football field away, so she wasn't worried about anyone seeing her, but it did make her uncomfortable. Flashes of lightning illuminated the gathering clouds above and she could see the storm was coming in the direction Chad would be driving, worrying her even more.

Becca walked back to the porch and opened the front door, stumbling sideways, as Homer tried to get inside. She jumped past him, denying the droop eared dog entry as the wind blew the door open before Becca could grasp the door handle. It slammed against the frame, making a noise like a shotgun blast. Homer tried again, but Becca put a foot out to shoo him away. He conceded defeat as he hung his head low and went back to the porch, allowing her the room to hook the door with her foot and slam it shut. The macabre dance coupled with all the noise, caused Toby to cry hysterically and Becca bounced him up and down, humming to soothe him.

"Shhh little one. Daddy'll be home soon," she crooned. "He'll want to hold you since he's been gone all week."

Toby shifted towards her, grasping her nipple so tight it caused Becca to wince in pain. She tried to ignore the hurt, biting her lip instead to distract her from it. After a couple of minutes, his sucking became lighter, and Becca felt him go limp against her as a pins and needles sensation crept up her arm. Holding Toby was getting uncomfortable, and she thought it may be a good idea to put him in his crib. All the jostling and noise was only making him irritable.

She rocked him gently for a few minutes, giving him time to calm down. Then Becca tip toed her way into the nursery and eased Toby into his bed. He stirred for a moment then rolled onto his side, curling up in a fetal position and sucking his thumb. She pulled a small blanket over her sleeping baby's legs, figuring she'd have a half hour at best before he woke up again. Becca tied her robe together and went to the end of the hall, then walked through the living room and into the kitchen. Her phone was on the countertop where she left it and she frowned when she saw it wasn't plugged in. Becca checked the battery life and grimaced when she saw it registered ten percent. She checked for messages from Chad and saw nothing there, no calls either. She tapped her foot in nervous anticipation, worrying over her absent husband and assuring herself he'd be home soon. While she was in there, she'd check the back door and make sure it was locked. The kitchen was dark, so she flipped the light switch on. The bulb flickered a few times, then went out.

"Damn, just my luck," she said aloud. She looked at her phone and spoke to the speaker, "hey, Siri. Turn on the flashlight."

The tinny computer voice assured her it was on, she held the phone in front of her, then started across the room toward the door. When she got there, she wiggled the handle and was relieved to see it was, in fact, locked. She peered through the door window, looking into the backyard where a pitch black sheet of darkness covered everything. The garden lay beyond the edge of the yard, Becca knew, but there was nothing but a line of trees after that. *Just as well.* She thought. *There's nothing to see anyway.*

Becca left the kitchen and walked back through the living room, then crossed the hallway to Toby's room. She took a quick peek in on her baby, watching him for a moment, as he lay in the same spot, sleeping and oblivious to anything around him. She smiled, then left his room and stepped across the hall to her bedroom where a large king-sized bed took up most of the area. The sheets and blankets lay crumpled and unmade across the mattress. Two nightstands sat on either side of the bed, both overflowing with unruly paper wrappers, a few soda cans, empty cups, and a small weather radio. Most of the junk was on Chad's side, of course, and she needed to tidy up the room before he got home. He never gave her a reason to think he cared, but it bothered her. She wanted him to come home to a clean house. Her husband took care of her after all, being gone all week. Even though Chad talked about how he wanted to work from home someday. He wanted the small twenty-acre farm they owned to be a working one, taking care of all their needs. Chad had lots of dreams, but Becca always agreed with him and never wanted to take those dreams away.

A man without a plan, can't dream too big. Another of her daddy's sayings and one she never divulged to Chad, but she could see him following her daddy's wisdom, whether her husband knew it or not.

The weather radio emitted a low droll of static mixed with occasional mechanical words from a flat computer-generated voice—much like the monotoned man on her daddy's old crank radio—giving warnings about the advancement of the storm. It creeped her out and she really didn't want to listen to it with Chad gone, but Becca thought it a good idea in case the storm produced any tornadoes. The radio squawked, picking up an octave and Becca reached over the bed, turning it down a notch, so it didn't disturb Toby.

She turned to the closet and opened the door, then searched through several garments and found the outfit she'd been saving for

Chad. It was a silky shirt and shorts, not extremely revealing but just enough to keep his interest and get the blood pumping. She tossed the clothes onto the bed and started to untie the robe, as a loud crash hit the front door. Becca jumped, emitting a small yelp as she did. Her heart thudded in her chest as she slowly tied the robe again and walked to the bedroom door, then eased her head into the hallway, speaking nervously.

"Chad? That you?" There was no answer. "Chad?"

The wind battered the side of the house with a heightened fury, the windchime eerily sang, keeping time with the torrent. There was no sound from Toby's room and thankfully the noise didn't wake him. Becca recalled the loaded shotgun Chad kept in the closet at the end of the hall was within reach and she figured she better retrieve it. Becca slowly inched toward it, keeping her eyes trained on the living room entrance as she put her back against the door and fumbled for the handle. When she found it, she eased the closet door open, cringing at the sound of the old hinges rubbing against each other. She paid no attention to the noise, but kept her eyes focused on the living room, hearing her heart thudding so loudly she thought it would burst her eardrums. Harsh breath exuded from her nostrils, the heat fogging her glasses. Strange, she thought, with all the noise, Homer wasn't barking. She figured he'd be going insane if someone were on the porch.

Becca grabbed the gun and started down the hallway toward the living room. Her body shivered with each step she took. She peeked in on Toby as she walked past his room and saw he was lying still, sleeping soundly. Becca turned her attention back ahead of her, as goosebumps rose on her flesh. She held the shotgun low, but ready, as the barrel of the gun shook up and down in cadence with the rhythm of her trembling body. Becca walked to the door and heard Homer whimpering from the other side.

"Homer?" she called, "Homer, what's wrong, buddy?"

The dog scratched furiously against the wood door, causing it to rattle in its frame. Becca didn't want to open the door and had no desire to see what was out there, but Homer needed her help. She held the gun with one hand and extended her other to the door handle, then took a deep breath and turned it. She eased the door open as lightning flashed across the sky, causing her to squint. The large bloodhound nearly knocked her down as he bolted inside, making a mad dash for the recliner. Becca almost dropped her gun but managed to hang on while Homer jumped in the seat behind her and curled into a ball. The dog shook uncontrollably, producing small whimpers and whines as he turned his head to look at her. His large dopey eyes pleaded with her to keep him safe while thunder rumbled overhead, shaking the house.

Becca stood there in disbelief at the protector of the house and how scared he was of the storm. It was then she realized the door was hanging open. Her hand went to the handle to slam it shut but stopped when she noticed a man standing at the edge of the porch. He stood statue still and she couldn't see his face but noticed the strands of hair whipping uncontrollably about his head. He had an air of familiarity, but Becca wasn't taking chances. She pulled the shotgun up in front of her. The robe fell open as she did, revealing her naked body to the stranger, but she didn't care. All that mattered was protecting her home and her baby.

"Get out of here," she shouted. "I know how to use this thing. My husband, who'll be here any minute, taught me." This was a lie, as it was her daddy who showed her how to use a gun, along with how to chop wood and a host of other things. She was a country girl who knew how to survive. "You best hit the road!"

But the figure made no effort to run. Becca slowly cocked the gun and put her finger close to the trigger. She pulled the gun tight against her shoulder and started to take aim when her glasses fell from her face and onto the floor in front of her. She instinctively tried to grab them, tilting the gun as she did and grazing her finger across the trigger. A loud blast permeated her ears and Becca stumbled backward, then fell to her bottom, off balance from the recoil of the gun. She dropped the weapon to the floor and was disoriented with her vision blurred from losing her glasses. She couldn't see if anyone remained on the porch due to the wind that blew through the front entrance, slamming the door against the wall. She saw it but heard nothing, only an incessant ringing in her ears. Becca's hair fell across her face, whipping into her eyes as she felt a gail force reminiscent of being in a wind tunnel. She fought against it, reaching her arm to the door, then rose to her feet and shoved her shoulder into it, slamming it shut. The door locked automatically, but she turned the deadbolt for good measure, then fell to her knees again.

Becca stayed there, trying desperately to regain her composure as she put her hands on the floor in front of her. She shook so badly, she thought she'd fall forward on her face. The noise in her ears was mixed with Toby's crying in the other room. It sounded like a distant calling with his screams and the thrum of noise from her damaged eardrums. The whole experience made her nauseous but she had to get to him. Without her glasses it would be difficult to navigate the house, but she didn't care. She knew this house well enough to get to his room blind or not.

She made her way, feeling along the wall, to her baby, listening as his crying intensified to solid wails with brief intervals of choked breath in between. Becca stumbled into Toby's bedroom, lunging for his crib. She felt the milk running down her chest in response to Toby's crying. She picked him up and pushed his head against her chest. He rooted furiously, latching onto her, and drinking ravenously, sucking for every drop of milk he could get.

Becca caressed his head, then took a deep breath and tried to regain her composure. *What the fuck was that all about? Was there someone there, or did she imagine the whole thing?* Becca walked with Toby attached to her, back to the living room with her entire body shaking. *What a country girl she turned out to be.* She thought. *Couldn't even manage to use a gun properly.* She needed to sit for a moment, but also needed to see if anyone was out there. She needed to call Chad to see if he was close so he could deal with whoever was out there. Becca reached for her pocket to retrieve her phone, pulled it out and pushed the home button, but nothing happened. She was staring at a black screen. The phone was dead and needed to charge, hell, she needed a new phone. The battery life on the old iPhone eight she owned was fleeting at best, never staying charged for long. She looked worriedly around the room, not wanting to go in the darkened kitchen—that much she was sure of—but not wanting to sit here and do nothing while a crazy man was outside. Homer was curled into the recliner, making no effort to move.

"Thanks for your help, you mangy mut," Becca muttered, as she went past him. She sighed, feeling bad about her words and gave him a pat on the head with her free hand. Becca felt nervous shivers convulsing through Homer's slender body. "It's okay, boy, I'm scared too."

Becca slowly bounced Toby rhythmically with her body with her ears still ringing, enhancing the sound of her fast beating heart. She needed her glasses to see outside effectively. She ran her foot along the floor, trying to find them, feeling for the frames with her toes. When she found them, she knelt while juggling Toby in one hand, and reaching with the other. She grabbed the glasses and put them on her head.

Rain fell in sheets against the window as streaks of light from outside illuminated the living room. She kept the overhead lights out, not wanting to bring attention to whoever was out there. Becca stepped to the window and eased back the curtain and realized she could see very little with the water blurring the glass, but she could still make out the edge of the porch. There was no one there and she laughed at the absurdity of her imagination as an irritating tinny ring pulsed from inside her ears.

Becca shifted Toby to one side, holding him with an arm that was half asleep, and eased the curtain back to its original position. Her shaking had calmed her enough to help Toby get back to sleep and she needed to get this robe off and put on some clothes. She went to her bedroom, taking Toby with her and laid him on the bed, placing pillows around him so he wouldn't roll off. He turned his head to the side, extending one arm beside him and curling the other by his head. She gave him a light kiss on the cheek, then pulled off the robe and threw it on the bed and grabbed the silky night clothes. Becca slipped into them, then checked herself in the mirror, smiling at the fit of the clothes, as they only accentuated the areas up top. Her best feature in her opinion. Her hips and belly weren't to her liking yet and she continued to hide it from Chad, even though she suspected he didn't care, but it bothered her all the same. Becca wanted to get her body back to her pre-baby days—had even gone to the effort of watching some YouTube videos for workout routines—but it all waned due to Toby's needs. Little else mattered than feeding and caring for him and all the rest would have to wait. She grabbed her phone from the robe and plugged it into the charger by the bed, then turned for her baby.

The weather radio squawked low in the background, reminding her of the imminent doom outside. The announcer's voice wasn't as frequent as it was earlier and she figured the worst of the storm, as evidenced by the wind quieting down, must have passed. Except for the radio, the house was eerily quiet. She picked up Toby, holding him close, and made her way into the living room, pushing Homer from the recliner. He gave a tired protest, then stretched, and walked to the corner to lie down. She figured she'd watch some TV to pass the time, maybe choosing some reality show to help her forget about the trouble she'd been through tonight. She fumbled through the side pouch of the chair until she found the remote, but before she turned it on, she shifted Toby to one side, freeing her hand to push the power button on the remote.

The television came to life but all she got was a blue screen with white lettering indicating no signal. She sighed, knowing the satellite bill was paid. The storm was the most likely culprit, but she'd check the TV just in case. Becca rose from the recliner and walked to the television set. The large rectangular object hanging on the wall was a testament to Chad's ability to get as many inches as possible across the living room wall. It was like being in a movie theater, and with the surround sound speakers adorning the room, it sounded like one. Becca thought it was a bit too much, but not Chad, as the television and all the accoutrements surrounding it, produced a sense of pride in her husband.

She looked to the back of the TV but saw nothing but a dark chasm with wires jutting from it. She'd have to turn the light on overhead if she were to see what was going on back there. Becca started for the light switch, but stopped when she heard a low static coming from the TV. She turned to look at the screen and saw black horizontal lines rolling from the top to bottom. A muffled voice came through the speakers, childlike and almost giddy. She recognized it immediately, because it was from her childhood. The sound of a purple dinosaur she knew very well.

I love you, you love me, we're a happy family. The sing-song voice rolled from the speakers, as Becca stared incomprehensibly at the screen. She stepped back, holding Toby close to her and shook her head. The voice continued to repeat the same words over and over, like it was caught in some infinite loop with the goofy chuckle prominent at the end of each cycle. She felt her legs getting weak, threatening to go out from under her, as she gave up and fell into the recliner. The tone of the voice began to change, becoming different than the laughing dinosaur. It was another she recognized and one she'd thought long forgotten. Christopher's voice came through the speakers. She listened in terror, trying to understand what was happening. She had no explanation though, as her brother sang louder with his voice off key. It burned in her mind and Becca wanted it to stop. She grabbed for the remote and pushed the power button. The TV continued and wouldn't turn off even though she pushed it again and again. Christopher's voice dug deep into her ears, taking over every sense of her reality while she shook her head side to side, trying to get relief, but her brother wouldn't be denied.

"Stop it, Christopher," she cried out. "Stop it!" The TV went silent, and the screen returned to blue. The no signal warning flashed poignantly across it as Becca stared at the screen. Her ears were still ringing from the shotgun blast and every fiber of her body shook. She brought her hand with the remote in it shakily forward to turn the set off. It responded this time and plunged the room into darkness, and she sat there quietly for a moment, jumping when Toby bit down on her tit. The whole spectacle seemed less bothersome to him, as he sucked furiously on her.

Her fear turned to anger, and she wanted answers. *Why was Christopher doing this? How could he be doing this?* The questions burned at the back of her mind. Becca turned her head toward the window. The rain had slacked off and fresh streaks of lightning flashed across the western sky. It was distant though and thunder followed a few seconds later, shaking the house lightly. She sat there thinking of what had transpired and how the thought of Christopher being around made her nervous. Had he been released, and her family failed to tell her? She didn't think they would, but she hadn't been in contact with them for a while, ignoring requests to visit with the baby.

She looked at Toby and saw he was sleeping soundly against her. The thought that maybe what she saw on the porch earlier was Christopher burned in the back of her mind. *Should she confront him?* He always prided himself as Becca's protector and big brother who stayed close during the storm. Chad was her confidant now, but he wasn't here, and she thought it odd how Christopher would suddenly show up. It was almost too convenient, and the thought did roll in her head that this wasn't her brother, but some other crude trickster. But who else but Chad and her family would know about him? She decided it was time to find out. In her wildest dreams she'd never think of going outside again, but she had to see if her brother was out there and put an end to this crazy shit. Becca stood from the recliner and carried her sleeping baby to his room, then laid him in his crib. The thought of leaving him here made her cringe, but she couldn't take him outside, not with the rain and cold to make him sick. Why she ever took him outside before was beyond her.

She left his room and walked toward the living room, then turned on the hall light to give her just enough light to see but not enough to disturb Toby. She walked to the front door, picked the shotgun up from the floor, and checked her glasses to make sure they didn't fall off again. Becca slipped on her fleece lined shoes by the door. Then placed the butt of the gun in her armpit and laid the barrel over her forearm, keeping the gun pointed low. She knew she'd have to pump it to get another bullet in the chamber, but for now, she'd keep it empty to avoid another misfire.

Becca looked sadly at the damage the gun had done to the floor, viewing the area in the low light of the hall. A blackened spot at least a foot wide stretched across the white carpet and fragments of fabric were strewn to the side, lying in shriveled heaps. She sighed, then switched the outside light on. Becca called for her valiant pooch and watched as Homer, tail between his legs, begrudgingly shuffled out of the corner, and stood beside her.

Becca smiled at him, "glad you decided to join me."

She opened the door and stepped onto the concrete porch, nervously looking around. "Christopher?" she said. "Christopher. If you're out here, show yourself." There was no answer, only the sound of light splatters of rain against the metal roof of the porch and the windchime singing its tune. She pulled the gun against her, extending the barrel out in front, then walked onto the driveway.

The wind blew her sheer clothing, pushing it against her body, causing her to shiver. The air was noticeably colder, as goose bumped flesh stood on her forearms, and she was suddenly glad she left Toby inside. She heard the front door creak, then shut behind her, clicking lightly closed. She thought about the door locking, but Becca wasn't concerned, as they kept a key under the flowerpot. She'd use it to open the door when she got back, confident Toby was safely locked inside, now away from danger. Becca ventured further and jumped when she heard a noise from the yard. Homer's ears perked up and his nose sniffed the air. She pointed the barrel toward the noise and saw a plastic grocery bag suspended from the branch of one of the bushes lining the driveway. She eased a little.

"That thing looks vicious," she said to Homer, "better not get too close."

Fuck this. Becca had had enough. Christopher wasn't out here, and it was time to go in and get some warm clothes on, then go to bed. She'd have Chad check on things once he got home. She started to turn but hesitated as something caught her eye near the entrance to the main road. The shadow of a man stood there. "Christopher?" she yelled. "Is that you?"

There was no answer. She heard a low growl emitting from Homer's throat. Becca went on alert, pulling the shotgun to level, balancing it on her hip, so she could free up one hand. She reached into her pocket to retrieve her phone so she could call 911, then realized the phone was inside charging, again. She cursed under her breath at her own stupidity, as Homer's growl turned to barking. Becca noticed his interest was now directed to something in the backyard, near the garden. Homer lobbed toward it, ears flopping, barking incessantly, and Becca turned her gun in the same direction but didn't follow right away. She looked at the area at the end of the driveway. Whoever was standing there before was gone, so she turned her attention back to her dog, following with nervous anticipation.

"Homer. Homer get back here you stupid dog," she called, in a loud whisper. Homer was too far ahead to hear any of her protests. "Fine then," she said.

She stepped into the yard and immediately felt water soak her feet. The cold muck made her teeth chatter and she cursed herself over the poor choice of footwear, wishing for the Muck boots sitting by the door in the house. She hadn't planned on being in the yard though. There was no turning back now, so she trudged forward, but then stopped, noticing Homer wasn't barking. She squinted through the darkness and could just make out his wagging tail, as he sat near the scarecrow Chad had built before he left for work.

Stupid dog. She thought. At least she didn't have to worry about stranger danger, as the hound would be going crazy if anyone was actually there. It was time to collect her dog and go into the house before she got sick.

The muddy water squished between her toes as she walked on, making her feet heavy. This was a low part of the yard that didn't drain well, and she could feel her feet sinking deeper in the swamp. A shoe came loose from her foot, but there was no way she'd find it in the dark. This only added to her uneasiness.

"Damn," she muttered to herself, "I liked those shoes."

Becca continued with one foot exposed to the elements and the other clad in a water-soaked shoe, offering no protection at all. A few more feet and she arrived at the edge of the garden. Homer stopped barking and came to her side, where he stood behind her whimpering, leaning his cold wet body against her sheer pants. The clothing offered no protection, and her feet were cold, chilling her to the bone. She shivered uncontrollably, and Homer's wet fur against her leg made it all worse. She wanted to go inside but couldn't shake the thought something was out here. Becca extended the gun in front of her, but she couldn't keep it steady as the barrel jumped up and down. She couldn't make out much and thought maybe her mind was playing tricks on her, but she thought she saw something in the dark.

She studied it further and realized it was only the stump of a tree Chad had been chopping on before he went on the road. His axe was still buried in the freshly sawn timber. There was nothing to see here. She looked at the sad eyed bloodhound sitting next to her and Homer let out fresh whines and pawed the side of her pants. Then grabbing ahold of the fabric with his teeth, he attempted to lead her away back toward the house.

"Homer? What on earth are you afraid of?" He nudged his nose on her leg. "What is it? What's got you spooked?" she said.

Homer lifted his head to sniff the air, and Becca instinctively pulled the gun tight against her shoulder. Light streaked across the sky, illuminating the area a few feet away. A dark figure stood there.

She screamed and stepped back. The sudden movement caused her to stumble. She fell to her bottom, losing the grip on the gun. The muddy ground soaked her instantly, making her feel as though she wet her pants. Becca paid no attention to it and scrambled to her hands and knees where Homer, already cowering, sat waiting for her. Panting and unable to catch her breath, Becca grabbed for her gun, but it was out of reach. She scrambled for it but stopped when she saw the feet of the man standing between her and the gun. Becca rose slowly, holding Homer for support, and stared the man in the eyes, as a fresh streak of lightning flashed across the sky. It was Christopher. He stood there with his face flat and unmoving, wearing a hospital outfit. She recognized it because she wore one similar when she was a patient, as memories of dark times flooded her mind. The desolation she felt with only Christopher to console her, to keep her sane. She'd left those days behind her, along with him, but her brother stood before her now, a testament to everything she'd tried to forget. He was holding Chad's axe in his hands and its presence could not be denied.

Christopher spoke in a low gravelly voice. "Becca. Why did you leave me?"

Becca shook her head slowly, as she shivered, standing in the darkness, exposed the elements. Her teeth chattered when she spoke. "Christopher? How...?" she trailed off.

He said nothing, only moved closer to her and then he spoke again. A voice reminiscent of something from the grave. A thing buried from the past. A ghost from a life long forgotten. "Becca. You didn't answer me. Why did you leave me there? You and me, we're a happy family."

She tried to speak, but the words were caught in her throat, because this wasn't happening, it couldn't be.

Christopher spoke again. "I was always there for you, but you left me!" he protested.

A pit rose in her stomach. Her mouth went dry, as the fear she felt became palpable. She tasted the heaviness in the air, knowing danger stood in front of her. She knew she was helpless to do anything. Homer growled, then let out a sharp bark.

"Homer, no!" Becca protested but it was too late, the dog was gone. She watched in horror as the axe rose in the air, coming down on her bloodhound protector. There was a *thunk* like a sharp instrument burying into a tree trunk and Homer made a quick whelp before silence, as cold and horrible as she could imagine, invaded the air. She watched, crying, as the axe lifted Homer's body into the air a couple of times. When the instrument wouldn't come free from the dog, Christopher put his foot on Homer's body and jerked hard to retrieve it, then he stood there, silently assessing the situation.

Becca wanted nothing to do with this. She whimpered, trying to keep her composure, but unsure of anything now. She turned for the house, running with all she had as the rain fell harder, soaking her shirt and pants. It felt like she had nothing on at all. Her body convulsed underneath her pretty clothes. All ruined by following her dog to his demise. Everything was ruined by her brother and tears welled in her eyes. The thought of Homer, of her life, she brushed it away for the moment, as she hurried to the front porch. Her foot slipped on the first step, and she fell to one knee, producing a gash on her skin.

Stinging pain crept up her leg, but she ignored it, crawling the rest of the way to the door, then turning the handle, and realizing the door was locked. Becca fumbled for the key under the flowerpot, shoving the thing to the side, causing it to crash against the floor, spilling dirt and terra cotta pieces everywhere. She found no key, as she desperately fished her hands through the area and ran her fingers through the dirt and debris, trying to find something that wasn't there.

"Fuck, fuck, fuck! It has to be here," she said aloud. She'd locked herself out before, but the key was always there. The back door, she'd have to try it, but how was she going to get there with Christopher running around? He was probably right around the corner, waiting for her. *How could he be here, after all this time?* The thought rolled through her, making her head swim, as she remembered his violent tendencies. She partly left him behind because he made her do evil things. Christopher was the bad kid, and she was the good one. Her mommy said so, but she didn't see it then because Becca was so engrossed in her brother; loved him unconditionally. She couldn't see what he was doing to her. With enough therapy, she finally saw him for what he was and thought he was gone forever, left to rot in that damned hospital, along with her feelings for him. But he escaped and now he wanted revenge for Becca leaving him. *Toby.* The thought crossed her mind like being hit in the face. She had to get to her son before Christopher did.

Standing on wobbly legs, Becca leaned against the door and took off the muddy shoe, so she wouldn't slip again, then walked to the corner of the porch. She peered into the yard, seeing how dark it was. Her teeth were chattering so hard, she thought she may bite her tongue off. She eased her way off the porch, staying close to the house. She stopped halfway to her destination and managed to stretch her head enough to look in one of the windows. The hall light was still on, just as she'd left it, but from her vantage point, she couldn't see Toby's room. If she were on the other side of the house maybe, but she couldn't go there now.

Becca was only a few feet from the back porch, but it might as well have been ten miles because her legs were so weak. She didn't know if they could carry her much farther and the cold permeated every part of her body, causing fresh chills to run through her. Her lips were quivering, and the wind picked up, blowing the falling rain against her soaked clothing, and adding to the discomfort. Her nipples peaked as well, and she felt rivulets of warmth coming through her nightgown. It was Toby's feeding time, and a feeling of dread came over her as she laid her head against the house. A faint noise came from inside and she heard Toby crying. She cried, realizing her baby was awake inside and didn't know where his mother, the only comfort in his life, had gone. It only added to her need to get inside as quickly as possible.

She gathered all her resolve and walked the last few feet to the back porch and clumsily made her way up the three steps and onto the small concrete slab. Her feet were muddy, and she had to walk slowly to keep her footing, but Becca managed to reach for the planter by the door. She knocked it out of the way and found a small key there. She picked it up, holding it close to her chest, like some trinket from a video game she used to play where the key would take you to the next level. Her hands shook uncontrollably as she brought the small piece of metal to the door handle, then eased the key into the keyhole. But before she could turn it, a cold hand grabbed her wrist.

A scream parted her lips and she fell, landing on her back, taking her breath for a moment. Becca scrambled for purchase on the concrete floor, scooting to the steps and falling, hitting her head as she descended. Sharp pain pierced the back of her head. Her consciousness threatened to fade, but it couldn't, she had to stay alert. She tried to focus as a shadowy figure leaned over her. She looked up to see Christopher with an axe in his hand. "Christopher, don't," she said with a weak voice, as her world began to fade.

Light flashed from the sky, illuminating the porch, as he smiled, turning his head slightly to consider her, lying on her back. He crouched beside her and whispered in her ear. "I've got you now, it'll all be okay."

Becca struggled to stay conscious, as darkness clouded her vision, and she fought the urge to go to sleep. It was too strong, and she finally succumbed.

When she woke her skull was pounding and she reached for her head, wincing from the pain when her fingers touched the cut on the back of her scalp. It felt as though a nice lump was swelling there. She pulled her fingers back and saw blood. Becca rolled to her side, shaking off the fog as best she could, then tried to get to her hands and knees. Her outfit was soaked through and her body shook uncontrollably as a wave of nausea hit her and she wretched the contents of her stomach onto the lawn. Becca rose to her feet on wobbly legs threatening not to hold her, and she stumbled forward, nearly falling. She managed to right herself, then walked up the steps of the back porch, using her hands to steady herself on the support post. The back door was hanging wide open, and blood trailed from the entrance and onto the porch. She saw bloody footprints off the side, disappearing into the darkness. Crimson colored handprints adorned the door facing, smeared like a morbid finger painting. She listened for her baby, but there was no crying. *Toby wasn't crying.*

"Toby!" she cried out. "Toby, mommy's coming."

Becca willed her feet to move, then stumbled forward, falling to her knees. She crawled through the open door and her pants leg caught a small nail jutting from the wood of the door facing. It tore through her clothing and sunk into the meat of her leg, and she fell to her back, crying out in pain. Tears burned her cheeks, hot and regretful, because her baby needed her, and she couldn't get to him. *Was there something wrong with Toby?* No, no, no, she wouldn't think it, didn't want to consider it.

"Toby! Toby, please. Cry for mommy, let me know you're okay."

Becca pulled herself to her knees and willed her body forward, crawling across the kitchen floor. A healthy trail of blood strung from behind her and mingled with what was already there, staining the kitchen floor. The ache in her head was dizzying, but she couldn't pass out again because Toby needed her.

The opening to the living room lay just within reach of her, at least what she could see of it in the shadowy room, as no lights were on. She couldn't find the strength to get to the switch and stumbled forward into the living room. Becca fell onto her outstretched hands and felt the carpet under her saturated with something sticky or muddy. It felt like she was stuck to the fabric of the carpet, like it was holding her down. It disgusted her and she tried to break free of its grasp, but only became more entwined with the muck below her.

Her hair clung to her face, but she couldn't pull it back, as her hands were mired in the gelatinous ooze on the floor. There was a coppery smell present near her nose and Becca couldn't stand it any longer. She wiped her face with her hand. Some of the liquid got into her mouth and a sudden feeling of repulsion took over her senses, causing her to gag, spitting the vile nastiness out as best she could. Becca threw her arms up, flailing them to the side and lost her balance, falling into the puddle beneath her. She immediately rolled to the side, only to feel more of the slime on her back. It crept under her shirt, sticking to her skin and she extended her arms forward, trying to gain purchase. There was an object in front of her covered in the same goop. It was round but not perfectly so, more of an oblong shape as best she could figure from only her sense of touch. She winced but used the object to help prop herself to her knees.

Becca fell against the wall and reached for the light switch, then hesitated for a moment. *Wouldn't the light alert Christopher of her whereabouts in the house?* It was too late to worry about him, Toby was her only concern. Thoughts flashed through her mind. Things she couldn't, wouldn't think about. *Why the fuck wasn't he crying? What the fuck is going on with Toby?*

Becca slowly flipped the light switch and the room flashed to existence. What Becca saw made her wail, as fresh screams escaped her lips. Tears fell mixing with the sticky ooze on her face and falling into her mouth. The taste of copper mixed with dirt invaded her tastebuds and her insides threatened to fall onto the floor as she stared forward into the room. Homer, what was left of him, lay sprawled everywhere. His headless torso curled up in the recliner and legs and entrails lay strewn out across the floor. His blood splattered on everything, even the walls, as if someone decided to paint the whole area with the remnants of her dog. Then Becca cringed as she pulled her hand away from the partially skinned head of her beloved pet. His glassy eyes stared in different directions. The result of the axe that split it in two. Her throat seized and she found it hard to breathe, hard to utter a sound, only small gasps of strangled noise.

Thoughts of Christopher flooded her head, as she remembered why she could never keep pets. It was because he killed them all, leaving strings of littered carcasses in the backyard. It was one of the reasons he was sent away in the first place and Becca helped him. She was an accomplice to his evil whims and had no way to cope with it. Becca remembered holding Christopher, letting him know it would be okay and she would go with him wherever he went. She promised to prop him up, and he did the same for her. But she left him and let him stay hidden away. The dirty little secret her family wanted to hide, as Clyde and Libby Holston swept him under the rug. They let Becca go down with him, but he was back now, and this was his revenge. He wasn't her family's burden anymore, but hers to bear. Becca and Christopher together forever.

She suddenly found it hard to stand and sank to the ground, then she remembered what she was doing. Toby needed her. *Why wasn't he crying? Why the fuck wasn't he crying?* Becca pulled all her strength, all the energy she could find deep down inside of her and eased her protesting body toward the hall, to where Toby awaited her, sleeping in his bed. *Why the fuck isn't he crying? Why the fuck isn't my baby crying?* The thought rolled around in her head, increasing the denial something was wrong with her baby. No, she wouldn't have it. *Why isn't he crying? Why the fuck isn't he crying?* She repeated it over and over in her mind, as tears rolled down her cheeks.

Her legs threatened to go out on her at any time, but she wouldn't let it happen and with shaky hands groped for the wall, smearing bloody prints on the wallpaper. Toby's room was around the corner, the lights were out, along with the hall light. Everything was eerily quiet. Even the soothing sounds device—The one with a mother's heartbeat—was silent. It was too quiet. *Why isn't he crying? Why the fuck isn't he crying? Why?* Her mind exploded with the question.

Becca stepped into Toby's room and willed her arm to reach for the light switch. Her heart thudded in her chest, as every fiber of her body shook. She wanted to flip the light switch on, but the fear of what she thought she'd see made it extremely difficult to perform the task. Her fingers groped for the small plastic protrusion, as her blood soaked fingers stuck to the switch plate. She massaged it, feeling the sticky goo on her hands, on every inch of her body. Becca hesitated for a moment, then flipped the switch up.

The room illuminated and Becca squinted her eyes at the sudden brightness. She stared incomprehensively at the scene before her. The crib was covered in blood. It ran down the sides and into the floor. A large pool of crimson liquid spread over the white rug covering the floor. It flowed like a river off the edge of the fabric and onto the hardwood floors. There were words on the wall, written in blood across the off-white wallpaper.

You and me we're
a happy family

She screamed, falling forward, landing on the side of the crib, her arms drenched in the blood-filled scene she knew all along awaited her. The crib teetered and fell sideways, emptying the contents inside and Becca was forced to stare at the bloody lump on the floor. She looked away and sobbed uncontrollably as her throat tightened, and she couldn't breathe. Her mind was reeling, trying to understand what was happening. As her shrill cries filled the house, threatening to shatter any calm there ever was, or would be, in her life again. She saw gashes on the side of the crib, then her eyes trailed to the wall, seeing what she knew would be there. The axe lay leaned against it with blood stained handprints smearing the hickory wood handle.

She fell onto her hands and knees, then onto her stomach. The pooling blood soaked through her clothes, turning the white fabric into nothing but a sticky rag, covering her body. She never wanted to get off the floor again, and wished all of it was gone, because Christopher had returned, and his evil knew no boundaries. Whatever calm Becca created with her new life, was now shattered in an instant and it was all because of her evil twin.

"I hate you, Christopher," she screamed out, as fresh sobs rose from her chest. Tears and snot mixed with blood rolled down her face and into her mouth. It was everywhere. *Blood, so much fucking blood.* The smell and taste of it produced a metallic sensation Becca thought she'd never experience again. Like the times Christopher threw the bloody animals on her, making her breath in the glorious passion he produced. All his taunts, letting her know where she stood with him, and the motherfucker wouldn't leave her. He wanted to control her, take her down a notch, and he knew where to strike; to cause permanent pain.

She heard a voice in the distance, someone calling to her; the sound faint but familiar, like a whisper on the wind. "Becca? Becca are you here?"

It was Chad. He'd finally come home, and she heard him cry out, a distressed whine, something out of place for a grown man. It seemed almost feminine, as he called her again. "Becca," he said, between the anguished screams, "what the fuck is going on?"

She felt him shaking her, but her disjointed mind couldn't comprehend him. She was somewhere else other than here. He picked her up from the floor and she held the wall to steady herself. She watched as Chad reached to the floor and grabbed the bloody lump of flesh. He cradled it in his hands, pulling it close to his face, then laying his cheek against it. She had no words for him, no way to comfort him as Becca listened to his sobs and saw his chest rise and fall with each hitched breath.

This wasn't happening, she told herself. *Why Christopher? Why did you do it?* The thought rolled in her mind, beating a path to her subconscious, threatening to destroy any resolve her mind could muster. With a weak breath she muttered, "It was Christopher."

Chad turned to her slowly. He looked at Becca with a strange fascination. Like she said something unbelievable, and his face flared with anger. Streaks of tears made paths through the already drying blood on his cheeks. "What did you say?" he wailed to her. "What the fuck did you say?"

She looked away and her gaze trailed to the wall where the axe lay. It was gone. Becca's eyes widened, as she saw Christopher holding the instrument high above Chad's head.

"Christopher, no!" she cried, but it was too late. The axe found purchase, hitting her husband's clavicle, splitting the bone with a sickening crack. Warm blood splashed Becca's face, causing her to wince.

Chad looked at her with surprise, as he dropped the lump he was holding, and it fell to the floor, splashing in the blood there. She watched as her baby's lifeless body rolled to a stop against the wall. Chad reached for the wound on his shoulder, as his mouth quivered, fighting to say something, but there was nothing to be said. Becca's mind fell into the dark place where Christopher stayed, holding her, cradling her fragile psyche in his arms. Rocking her the same way she did Toby, but with more blood. *So much blood.* The thought left an egregious whelp, smacking her over and over.

Christopher placed a foot on Chad's chest, using it for leverage to pull the axe free, then he raised the instrument of death high again and let it fall to the middle of Chad's face. The audible crack of bone burned a hole through Becca's eardrums, and she cried, shaking her head. *So much blood, too much blood.*

Her mind reeled, as the axe came down again and again, hitting its mark over and over, turning Chad's head into mush. Pieces of brain matter splattered onto her husband's shoulders, then onto the floor, with each withdrawal of the instrument. Blood sprayed in fountains all over the room, turning the serene white landscape into something vile. Christopher screamed in delight. "You and me, we're a happy family," he said every time the axe fell into Chad's skull.

He finally stopped and looked at Becca with eyes that were crazed and distant. A mirror of her, as they were twins and looked so much alike but were so different too. Becca watched him, stared into his eyes to see what was there as an image flickered in her mind, and she realized she was looking at the mirror on top of the chest of drawers. She stood there, studying the reflection between the streaks of blood running off the glass and the bloody axe in her hands. Blood dripped from the tip of the blade as she spoke, but it wasn't her voice she heard, it was Christopher's.

"I've got you now. You don't have to worry about a thing, Becca. We're a happy family. The way it was always meant to be."

The End.

Within Me

Hurt

My relatives stare at me in disbelief. Like I'm a ghost from a tainted past, they'd tried to bury, now resurrected from the cold death perpetrated on me. I look to the floor and see clumps of black dirt, dripping from my rain-soaked hair. I glance at the wall beside me and see the grinning portrait of my grandfather staring back at me. I smile at the fact he thought he'd silenced me, but he was wrong. I was placed under the casket of the master himself and I felt the weight of the box crushing me. Old Grandpa Silas was six feet under, but his granddaughter was deeper and face down in the mud. I suppose they did know what they were doing though. If I didn't possess this power, there would have been no escape. But I made my way out and I'm stronger than my uncles and cousins thought. I'm Harper Lansing, descendant of the Lansing witches, and I'll end my family's reign of terror tonight.

I watch them scheme and contemplate their next move and remember how I got here, as the journey was nothing short of miraculous. All my family can trace their roots to Old Salem, during a time of upheaval and mistrust. The trials ended the lives of many witches, but my family escaped because of our powers, and to this day we are forever gifted or forever cursed. I like to think of it as a gift because powers like mine only show up occasionally, skipping a generation or two. All the Lansing witches had some gift, but few were like mine and I didn't even know about it until it manifested when I turned fourteen. As if puberty and all the other things a teenage girl goes through aren't bad enough, I was faced with something I had to hide. This concept wasn't foreign to me. You see, I have a disease called borderline personality disorder. My therapist told me it was because of the emotional losses in my life. My father for one. I lost him in an accident several years ago and have never fully dealt with my grief, as I was too young to remember him. My mom had trouble dealing with his death as well, hiding away most days in her room, making me feel alone in this world. As a result, I cut myself to release all my emotional baggage I suppose, acting out against a fucking world that hated me.

I'd been doing it for a couple of years, opting to cut instead of taking the meds that brought me down, as I felt they turned me into a zombie with no feeling at all. The day I discovered my powers, my friend, Sally, was staying over. She was sleeping in my bed when I got up to go to the bathroom. While in there, I started cutting my inner thigh and jumped when I heard a scream in the next room.

I ran in to see Sally sitting bolt upright, grabbing for her leg, crying out in pain. I turned on the bedside lamp and saw blood everywhere, coming from a cut on the inside of her leg, the same place I cut myself only moments ago. I took her to the bathroom to help her clean and bandage it and after I did, I checked my leg. There was nothing there, as the cut had vanished completely. The only thing I saw were the scars from previous cuts I'd made. I realized that day I possessed something special. The ability to place hurt on others after first harming myself.

At first, I feared my power because I didn't understand it and had no one to confide in. I wanted to show it off but didn't, mainly because I was too afraid of the consequences. You see, my brother was sent away after he started a fire in my grandpa's garage. Everyone was tightlipped about it except when my grandpa came by the house to tell my mom. I heard him inquiring about me as well and spied my mom shaking her head in denial about something. I had no idea at the time and remember watching as she ran to her room. I listened to the soft muffled crying through her door and figured it would only cause her more grief if I told her about me and my cutting, my powers, and all the things going on in my life. It was better to keep it to myself.

A couple of years passed, and I found myself in high school with very few friends. School, for me, was tough. I was never one to fit in, picking the path of least resistance, and acting out when asked to do something I hated. I never tried out for sports, or any school club and I only wanted to be left alone. I was content to be invisible in my everyday encounters and fuck those who got in my way. Sally Gentry was my only friend, and I liked it that way and my chosen status caused me to make enemies. Not that I tried to make the popular girls mad at me, but I suppose I had a bullseye on my back and Stacy Bozeman had a need to make me her favorite target. She made my life a living hell and always derided me, saying mean things to me all the time. This had been going on for a few years and started innocently enough when I'd walked by in the hall during my sophomore year of high school. I'd been a spec before then, staying the way I wanted to, out of sight of everyone. Then, out of nowhere Stacy started barking off insults. "Who the fuck you think you are, Lansing?" she'd say, then look at her friends and laugh. "You think because of your family, you're special?"

I tried to move on past her, but she would grab me by my backpack and use it to sling me into the lockers. The noise was loud enough to send all heads turning in the hallway. One time, my teeth slammed together so hard, I bit my tongue, filling my mouth with blood. I heard someone close by cry out in pain and I saw a kid running toward the bathroom, holding his mouth. This was earlier and my powers were still new. I hadn't learned to control them yet and I suppose I was manifesting everywhere. I wanted to direct the pain at Stacy but couldn't figure out how, so, I punched her instead. Blood poured from her lip, she grabbed my hair, then screamed in pain, as she suddenly let go and shook her head, massaging her scalp. She stared at me like I was something from outer space.

"Who are you anyway?" she said, then turned away with the rest of her friends.

I never understood Stacy. She came from money just like I did, although she exuded an air of perfection I could never possess. The Bozeman's were an old family in the Massachusetts area for many centuries and for reasons I didn't understand at the time, they made enemies with my family. There were rumors of an age-old feud between them, going back many years, stemming from a power struggle between the two families. Nowadays, they were together, and the Lansing-Bozeman corporation was a big conglomerate of production materials in the area. But deep down they were evil to the core and always plotting ways to take out the undesirables in their family. Stacy, I was sure, had a vendetta against me, and I suspect it came from our families past indifferences. But no matter where her feelings derived from, I took Stacy's bullying personally. Maybe too much.

The transgressions against me went on until my senior year of high school, sometimes with me striking back, and other times not, until one day Stacy was on a particularly heightened rampage. This was the day I snapped, deciding I'd had enough. I'm not sure what brought it on, maybe another busted lip I'd given her, but she had it for me worse than usual. She stepped through the school yard into the other nobodies, parting them like Moses at the Red Sea, along with her band of mean girls, all decked to the nines with designer apparel. I sat with my dark clothes, black fingernails, and dyed black hair; the least of the drabble in the hierarchy of my private school.

I remember listening to something about the bodies hitting the floor, when she grabbed my earbud and yanked it from me, throwing it across the pavement, smiling as wickedly as possible when she spoke to me.

"Who the hell are you?" she asked smugly.

I looked at her confused, as she knew who I was, but I wasn't sure if she wanted me to say it, or if this was a snide retort hurled at me as an insult. I was sure the latter was true, and I sneered at her, then spoke up, "I'm nobody, just a girl."

Stacy laughed, along with her entire crew. "You mean you don't have a name? What kind of fucked up shit is that? You expect us," she said, waving her arm wide to encompass the area around her friends, "to believe that we don't know your name? That you're a nobody?"

I slowly rose from my spot and walked to retrieve my earbud near the grass, but as I stooped to pick it up, Stacy planted a boot on my rear and pushed. I fell forward onto the grass, arms splayed before me, as Stacy and all her friends laughed. The rest of the kids in the yard joined in as well and the whole place was roaring with laughter, at my expense. I picked myself up and looked at her smug face, waiting, I suppose, for me to swing. I didn't give her the satisfaction of a reply, although the urge was great to cut deep into my arm, right there in front of her, bleeding Stacy to death. I'd been practicing with the use of my powers by then, trying them out on some unsuspecting kid or even an animal—strangely they worked that way as well—but wasn't sure if I could accurately direct them to Stacy, so I kept my composure. There were too many eyes on us anyway. I would get my revenge, but not here. "Stacy, I don't want trouble," I said. "Just leave me the fuck alone."

She turned to her comrades and said, "See, I told you she was nothing. You all think the Lansing's are a family to be afraid of." She pointed to me, never turning around, "they're no tougher than the rest of us." Then Stacy turned to me. "You brought this on yourself, bitch. Stay out of my way, freak, or I'll make your life a living hell. Got me?"

I glared at her, wanting to cut my throat right in front of her and make her bleed while she gasped for air. But even if I could, everyone would find out the truth about me. It was best they didn't know, didn't suspect me or I'd become a statistic like my brother, who I hadn't seen in years and thought I may never see again.

I left the school yard with rage burning in me to do something to Stacy. I didn't go to my next class, opting instead to brood on my predicament in the back of the school building. A place I could hide from everyone. I knew in another hour it would be time for my physical education class. It was a required credit, but I never participated, as I had a constant excuse, given to me by my mom to get out of it. I had the condition of anemia and couldn't be overexerted. It wasn't true, but I rarely saw sunlight and my skin was unusually pale, so I managed to get by with the lie. There would be no anemia on this day because blood would spill in great rivers with all of it directed at one person.

I snuck into class late and sat in my usual place on the bleachers where I was a speck no one paid any attention to. This made it much easier to vanish into the darkness below the seats. I went there and eased into a place where I could see the gym clearly through the bleachers. I directed my energy at Stacy as she bounced around the floor with her tight top and hair and makeup just right. As I watched her, the urge to hurt her became stronger. I wanted her to feel a physical pain as severe as the emotional pain she'd caused me. I'd never felt such anger and all my ire was directed at her, as a vindictive evil came over me; one that boiled from somewhere I couldn't pinpoint.

The worst I'd ever done to inflict self-harm was to cut myself around my upper thigh where no one could see, but that wasn't good enough. I wanted Stacy to suffer. I wanted to break her, and to do that, I first had to break me.

Watching Stacy through the bleachers, I could see her getting ready to serve the ball. She was waiting for the others to ready themselves for the game, standing at the edge of the gym, oblivious to me watching. This was my opportunity, but I needed leverage. I didn't know how much, as this was something I could never have imagined doing, but extreme measures were called for. I placed my arm between the base of the bleachers and the railing holding them up. I pulled a book from my bag and bit into the edge of it, then took a deep breath. I concentrated on Stacy, focused all my anger there, then stood and tried to break my arm, letting the weight of my body do the work. I felt my arm give, but not enough to break the bone. I managed to produce a small cut on my skin, but that was all. I looked through the bleachers at Stacy, focusing on her arm. I saw it bleeding, but only a small amount, one she didn't even notice. But at least it gave me the knowledge to know this would work, I only had to come up with a better way.

I looked behind me and saw a small folding chair. I grabbed it and placed it under the bleachers, then stood on it and centered my arm again. I was in a place of deep turmoil and the rage I felt from my father's accident coupled with the pain of my brother leaving, all boiled in me. I took a deep breath and kicked the chair from under me and felt the weight of my body come down hard on my arm. This time, I heard the bone underneath snap, and the pain was instantaneous, as hot tendrils shot through my arm. Fire seethed in me, from my wrist to my elbow and my vision became clouded with dots. I wanted to cry out from the pain, but instead bit down harder, as the hurt and anger fed on one another.

I heard Stacy screaming, as the glorious sound echoed throughout the gym. I wanted to look out and see the damage I'd inflicted on her, but I found myself staring at my arm instead. A jagged bone jutted from the skin, open, and gushing blood, as it poured down my arm and onto the floor. A splintered piece of blood-soaked bone stuck out just below my elbow and my wrist was twisted into an unusual shape. My hand lay dangling, lifeless and unable to move as the skin around it was red and seething with anger. I'd never seen anything so hideous, and I felt sick as waves of nausea overtook me. The dots were starting to connect, and I felt myself waning, my eyes rolled back, and the world around me went black.

When I woke, I saw blood around me, but my arm was as good as new, as though nothing ever happened to it. The wrist was straight, and the fingers moved as they always did and there was no bone sticking from the skin or scars or anything to tell I was hurt in such a horrible manner. I made my way to the top of the bleachers, looking for Stacy but she wasn't in the gym. I heard someone calling my name and looked to see Sally waving to me from the floor. I walked from the bleachers to meet her.

I noticed her lip had been cut and wondered if she'd been in a fight on my behalf. She gave me a concerned look. "Where have you been? You missed all the excitement. Did you hear about it?"

I shrugged, feigning ignorance. "No, what's up?"

"Stacy Bozeman broke her arm in PE class," she said, pointing across the gym. "Over there. A stray ball came flying from the dodge-ball court and knocked her down." Sally's eyes widened, as she told the story with more emphasis. "She fell on her arm and broke it. The gym teacher said she'd never seen anything like it. How someone could have received a nasty break from a fall like that." She shook her head and shivered. "The bone popped out of her arm. It was so disgusting. I doubt she'll ever be the same again."

I looked at her, thinking I should've been surprised over the event. Shocked like she was, but instead of being concerned for Stacy, I directed mine to Sally. "What happened to your lip?"

She touched her mouth, then looked at the floor. She sighed, "I guess I had a run in with Stacy's friends."

I hugged her and she pulled away at first, but then accepted my offer. I said the only thing I could think of at the time, "Thank you. You're a true friend, Sally. Fuck Stacy and the rest of them."

I released her and stared at her probing eyes. I'll never forget the look she gave me. Deep down I knew she suspected I had something to do with Stacy's freak accident, but I didn't care. I turned from Sally, making my way to the next class, trying to convey the same solemn look as everyone else in the school at the awful news of a classmate falling and hurting herself, but I couldn't stop smiling.

I started for home after school and noticed some of Stacy's friends were following me, so I picked up my pace, trying to find a place to duck into. I heard one of them yelling. "Hey, freak! We want to talk to you. I know you had something to do with Stacy. You better run. When we catch you, you'll be in worse shape than her!"

I felt my heart racing, feeling as though it would leap from my chest and knew I had no chance of getting away from them. They'd catch me before I made the turn up ahead. I had to slow their progress, so I reached into my book bag as I ran, retrieving a mechanical pencil. Thankfully, my mom only bought the best. They were all metal and heavier than your typical pencil. I stopped, kicked my shoe off, and rammed it into the top of my foot.

"Ow, shit!" One of the mean girls cried out.

I turned to see the lead girl on the ground, grabbing her shoe, as blood shot from the pencil sized hole in the top of her foot. I laughed, watching as one of the girls stopped to check on her. The others were still coming, so I turned and tried to run. My foot was healing, but it still hurt, making my movement slow and cumbersome. The best I could manage was a wounded hobble and I knew the other girls would catch me for sure at this pace. I took the pencil and jabbed it into the meat at the top of my leg, planting the thing as deep as possible. It had the desired effect, as another girl fell onto the concrete sidewalk, rolling from side to side. Blood stained her pants, producing a large dark spot. I pulled the pencil out of my leg, trying to stay upright, as the pain pulsed through my body. Pools of sweat formed on my forehead, and I wiped it with the back of my hand while I tried to line the pencil up to my other leg and sink it in to take another girl out, but I didn't have the strength to do it.

As I limped along, one of the girls caught up to me. She grabbed my wrist and pulled back, twisting it. She was bigger than I was and had more strength and in my weakened state, I had no way to fight her off. I couldn't concentrate and wasn't able to turn the pain on her.

I tried to bring the pencil up again for my leg, but she pulled me off balance and I fell onto my bottom. She immediately started kicking me in the ribs. My foot and leg were healing, the hurt there was nearly gone, but the stinging strikes to my ribs were replacing any relief I was feeling. The blows were coming so fast, I had no time to redirect them, so I put my arms over my head for protection, but the assault kept coming. She finally stopped, breathing heavily from exhaustion, as some of her friends stood by her now.

I looked up at her, watching her nostrils flare like a mad bull and her chest rise and fall in rapid succession. "What's you going to do now, freak?" She taunted me, as the girls around her laughed. "Stacy told us about you and your family. The whole bunch is a shit show." Then she said something to give me pause. "Even your brother. That freak burned down his grandpa's garage." She crouched beside me. "I heard flames came from his fingertips." She shook her head, "I don't know what kind of magic tricks you assholes know, but this time it won't work. We have you right where we want you and we're going to fuck you up, freak."

She stood, then took a deep breath and motioned to her friends. This was it. They were ready to finish me off and I didn't have the ability to stab myself, but I had another idea. I balled my fist, and using the side of it, punched myself in the nose. The sensation was like my sinuses exploded, as my eyes watered and I felt my nostrils fill with blood and build pressure, then let loose, running down my face and into my mouth. I leaned my head to the side and spit frothy red liquid onto the ground. The girl standing over me stumbled backward, grabbing her bleeding nose, as blood stained the front of her shirt and pants. The other girls went to her aid, and I took advantage of the momentary distraction to rise to my feet and limp for the alleyway. I slipped through the other side, as my legs had healed enough for me to hobble all the way to my house.

When I got there, the only thing left of my wounds were the rips on my clothing. My nose still throbbed but it was getting better. I felt it to make sure it wasn't broken. Not that I would've known what that sensation felt like. I'd had so many different feelings of pain that day, I doubted I could pick just one. I walked through the door to see my mom sitting on the couch. I watched as she looked at my clothing, frowning at the rips in my pants. She shook her head. "Those uniforms aren't cheap you know."

I shrugged. "It's the style I'm going for, I should've told you I guess."

She frowned, then sighed. She looked at me curiously. "What happened to your face?"

I turned away. "Nothing. I'm fine. Going to my room."

I headed up to my bedroom and laid back on my bed, breathing deeply. I looked up at the posters on the wall with the various rock stars on them. I looked curiously at the *Harry Potter* collection I kept from when I was a kid. The witches in those books lived ideal lives to mine. I had to feel good though about the small victory I managed today. *I took out Stacy and her friends today.* The thought of it made me feel like a superhero and I could feel the bruises on my side already healing. I took off my shirt and stared at them, watching as they went from purplish blots to the color of my regular skin. My bruised nose was healing as well, and I figured all signs of them would be gone by morning. I decided to go to bed early that night, as the trials of the day had taken their toll and I was feeling fatigue overtake my body. I needed rest. I got out of my clothes and put on my night gown, then got into bed, pulling the blanket up under my chin. I had a euphoric feeling, at least for now anyway.

The next day I got up at my usual time with the alarm pulsing in my head. I slept for nearly ten hours supposing the events of yesterday had taken their toll on me. I hopped out of bed and got ready for school, putting on a fresh uniform, then descended the stairs. My mom stood by the door, blocking my path with a steaming cup of coffee in her hand. "Hey, I think we should talk."

"Mom, I have to get to school before I'm late," I protested.

She gave me a mournful look. Her face was troubled, and it made her look aged beyond her years. "This won't take long. I got word from the principal that some things happened yesterday, and some girls were hurt. They said you had something to do with it. Is it true?"

I shuffled my feet, trying to think of something to say, but decided to come out with it. "They deserved what they got. They're so mean, I had to do something."

She let out a haggard breath, then motioned for the couch. "Let's sit."

I did and she sat beside me, setting her coffee cup on the table in front of the couch. She put her head in her hands. "I thought it would skip you, I hoped it would, but here we are." She put her hands to her knees and straightened them. Long, ropey veins protruded from her forearms like her blood pressure was up. It probably was and the trouble I caused her would be enough to do it. "How long have you known you had the ability to do what you did?"

"A few years ago, when Sally stayed over." I almost told her about my cutting but thought it may be too soon. The last time she and I had that conversation, I had to see a therapist and take anti-depressants. I suppose I should still be taking them but hadn't been for a while. Any one of those things could cause apprehension for the woman and she had enough on her plate as it was. I opted to stretch the truth a bit. "I accidentally cut myself in the bathroom and heard her scream. She couldn't figure out how it happened and still doesn't know."

My mother shook her head. "That makes sense. The power usually manifests after a stressful episode. That's why you were on meds before, because of your personality disorder, but also because it suppresses everything. If your power is as strong as I think it is, then you've stopped taking your medicine."

I looked at her surprised. She really did know me better than I thought. "Yes," I said weakly, "I quit taking my meds a long time ago. How do you know all this?"

She looked me in the eye. "You're my daughter and I know when you're hurting. I see the trouble in your face, Harper." She took her hand and extended it to my head, then brushed my hair back with her fingers. "You have the power of transference. The ability to place your pain or hurt or even love on another. It's a very potent ability. Were there any other incidents? Other than with Sally and the one yesterday?"

I nod slowly, looking away. I return my gaze to her. "What did the principal say? How many girls were reported hurt?"

My mom's eyes widened. "Stacy Bozeman is the only one he said anything about. What else happened?" I looked away, but she grabbed my chin and made me turn to face her. "Harper. This is serious. I can't let you go around doing damage. It'll get back to..." her words trailed off. The deep lines around her eyes enhanced the concern there.

I tilted my head, considering what she said. "Get back to who, mom?" I studied her face and saw a terrible pain there. Something had her deeply troubled. "Is it Grandpa Silas?"

She looked away, as if she were trying to choose her words carefully. "I don't want to scare you, but there are people within our family who will seek you out if they know what you are. Silas is one of them. They can never know. If they do, we could all be in danger."

I looked at the floor then went back to her, remembering the day Grandpa Silas came to the house. "Is that why, Matt went away?"

I'll never forget the look on her face. She stared at the wall. Her face was as white as the paint there. "Matt was a different situation. The wrong people found out about him. He has attention deficit syndrome with hyperactivity. Mental illness runs in our family. It isn't a bad thing, but a way for us to express ourselves in unique ways. Our powers can take us down bad pathways because of it sometimes," she sighed. "Matt for example. Impulse control is not his strong suit. He was angry and his pyrokinesis burned down your grandpa's garage. If he were allowed to go farther, it could've resulted in damage unimaginable."

Pyrokinesis. The thought lingered in my mind of what the mean girl said. Matt had fire come from his fingertips and she thought it was a trick. After yesterday, she may have figured out, the Lansing's don't play tricks. "Where is Matt?"

She shook her head, as fresh tears formed in her eyes. "He's been institutionalized."

I gritted my teeth and could feel the anger welling inside. He was like me, only unlike me, and Grandpa Silas knew about him. After my run in with Stacy and the mean girls, he'd find out about me as well. The thought came to me that Silas had connections and who knew how many were at the school alone? I suppose I could see what she meant by danger, but I had another burning question and I presented it to her with genuine inquisitiveness. "Mom, what am I?"

She let out a long breath, putting her hand to the corner of her eye and wiping. "You and I come from a heritage, dating back to before things were chronicled. We've been called magicians, demons, cursed banshees, supernatural beings, but typically were called witches."

I gave her a sideways glance as this was the first time I'd heard the title uttered. It gave me pause. "Witches? Like Sabrina or Hocus Pocus?"

She sniffed and smiled at me. "No, not the same at all. We don't conjure spells or dance under the full moon or anything. There's nothing dark about witches. People like to make us out to be evil because they don't understand who we are, the good we can accomplish in this world." Her eyes were wet as she looked at me. I saw the love there and the anguish as well. "They only want to squash us like bugs because they fear us." She took a breath, and looked at me, the words were becoming a struggle to get out. "There are times in history when fear becomes a frenzy. Religious zealots who are bent on destroying things they are afraid of. The Salem Witch Trials to be exact. We had relatives there. Luckily a few escaped before we were all killed." She reached for my hand and held it in hers.

"Some of our relatives were drowned or put in all manner of torture devices. There was one telling of a witch with powers like yours, whose throat was cut after being tortured and assaulted. She was thrown into a small grave and forgotten about, but her body healed itself and she dug out from the ground. The girl's name was Julia Lansing, the same as mine and she was your great grandmother. She lived a long time and kept our line going," she frowned. "Others weren't so lucky."

My mother looked into my eyes, and I saw the deep hurt there, as it provided a window into her feelings. The telling of these stories genuinely pained her. "We've been through other trials as well. The one I remember best was in the late nineties. There was a convent of witches outside of the city of Salem and I was part of their rank. We had a hospital where we helped underprivileged people; the people who had nowhere to go," she paused and smiled. Her demeanor changed and I could tell it was a good memory. "We didn't want money. We used our talents to help people asking nothing in return. Your father was among them, as well. He was the founder of the group and I fell in love with him the moment we met."

I thought about this, we lived in New England, only a couple of hours from Salem. I remembered going there one Halloween and it wasn't anything I expected. More show than sustenance. But to think we were connected to the bloody history of the place, made me even more curious. "We come from the heritage of Salem? We studied it in school, but I never heard our family mentioned."

She gave me a weak smile. "Harper, there are lots of things you don't understand and never will I'm afraid. The people who survived Salem vowed to stay in hiding, no longer showing people what we could do, only using our powers if we needed to. There was good reason to do so. Some witches use their powers for evil. That is a different sect altogether. If you're ever in contact with them, don't be fooled, they're wolves who hide behind the precipice of something truly evil."

I pondered this and wanted to ask more but continued listening instead.

"But not our family. We chose a higher path, as many became healers and helpers, along with other witch families, in hospitals and nurseries, only giving aid if it was needed, hiding the real reason someone was able to survive a particular infliction. Your father was among them." I could see the warmness in her face when she talked about him. "His name was Samuel Petra, or just Sam to all his patients he healed."

I smiled at her. It was then I realized, I barely knew his name and knew nothing about the man. It saddened me to think of my father as this great man who was buried from me; an enigma to be revered or pitied, maybe both.

She went on, "When we met, I was only eighteen, and I fell for him instantly. He had a light in him few possess. He was much older, but it didn't show." She smiled, laughing lightly. "When I say he was older, I mean he was at least fifty years my senior, yet he looked like he was only a year or two older than me," she looked at me warmly. "He had the same abilities you do. You, your father, and grandmother are the only witches I've ever known to have it. Your grandmother lived a long life, working as a nurse for nearly one hundred years. Your father would have too, I suppose if things had been different."

A light flashed in my eyes at the thought of living longer, and then another thought dawned on me, and I asked my mother about it. "Do I have the ability to heal people along with my transference abilities?"

She looked at me with pridefulness, but I could see the deep-seated worry underneath. It was like she wanted to say something she couldn't and acted as though her words hurt her as much as they made her happy.

"I don't know, but more than likely, yes. We can all heal others, it's an ability that makes us unique, but some of us, like you I suspect, can also heal themselves. It's why I think Samuel and your grandmother lived such long lives. You're special in ways you don't even know, and so far, you only see your abilities to hurt others, because you've been hurting yourself for so long. The illness you suffer, skews your way of thinking, makes you impulsive, like your brother." She looked away, then back to me, considering her words. "His impulsiveness is misguided though. It's why he burned down the garage." She shook her head, as she was clearly troubled by the thought. Then she looked at me, "I have something to show you."

She turned and concentrated on the coffee cup in front of her and it started to move slowly across the surface, stopping at the edge. "This is my power. It's called telekinesis and it's much weaker now because I'm out of practice. It manifested not long after I was diagnosed with depression in my teens and I take my medicine to keep the power contained within me, where its safe."

I looked at her with awe and trepidation over the fact she tries to contain her power and what horrible things in her past caused her to think that way. "Does anyone know about this other than me?" I asked.

She sighed. "Yes, many in my family do, your grandpa among them," she took a breath. "When I told you your father died in an accident, that wasn't true. His death was made to look like an accident. You see, we thought we were immune to the old ways, even had a sense of false security about the modern world. We no longer thought hiding our abilities was necessary." Her face crinkled and she sniffed as her eyes moistened. "Silas is partnered with some very powerful people. They found out about our free clinic, as word got around about the miraculous healings happening there. People called it angelic, a gift from God, but Silas and his people understood what was going on and they wanted to put a stop to it, as they were guided not only by their hatred but also greed. A free clinic did nothing to help the local health corporations."

I stared at her uncomprehendingly. "I always thought Grandpa was just a mean old man, not wanting to talk to any of us because he wanted to be alone or wanted things his way. I didn't know he had a network behind him."

"He plays the role of unassuming well, always preferring to hide from the public, using his wealth and influence. But when he wants something done, he has the people to do it. They're called Concilio Venatorum, originally. It's Latin for Council of the Hunters, and it formed many years ago in response to the witch presence or perceived threat of them. They went after some of the evil witches at first, mostly in Europe, but found it was easier to attack the good witches instead, starting in the early colonial period of this country. Their intentions are misguided. My brothers who have no powers, are in it."

I looked at her, as my curiosity peaked. This was a side of history I'd never heard. "This is crazy, mom. So, not everyone in our family has powers, and they're all witch hunters?"

She nodded. "Right, only some of us and the others try to contain the ones who do. My father has been instrumental in keeping the witches in the family under his watchful thumb. He only has the ones outside of our family killed. He finds ways to deal with us instead, showing a kind of mercy because of our bloodline." She shutters. "It's more like a modern torture though, always medicating and institutionalizing us. His way of a humane inquisition, I suppose. When were good, like I've been, we get to leave the hospital and stay in a house of his choosing," she waves her hand around, "like this one."

"Why do you let him do that to you? Why not just run away?" I said in protest.

She raises her head and lets out an exasperated breath. "I have nowhere to go, Harper, and back when I first came here, I had you and your brother to raise. I had no choice but to come here and stay and for my children, I'd make the same choice any day."

I smiled, feeling the conviction of her words, but then thought to myself. *Where do I fit into all this?* "When I get older, will Grandpa let me leave?"

"I don't know the answer to that, Harper. He's an old man, and probably doesn't have much time left and my brothers, unfortunately, are gaining influence in the organization. If they take over, I'm sure they won't be as even handed as he is because they are much more violent when they deal with things." She looked me directly in the eye, "I'm afraid they may want us dead."

My eyes widened. "Do you think they know about us?"

She looked at the floor, clearly regretting saying anything. "I'm sure they know about Matt and definitely me, but they may not be aware of how powerful you are." She smiled, trying to give me as much reassurance as possible. "Harper, you need to understand, the council is a group from several families, ours included, who weren't gifted with powers. There were people in the other families who exhibited powers long ago, but they were wiped out; taken away the minute they exhibited any signs they were a witch." She patted my hand. "Your grandpa would only lock his family away, like he's done Matthew and me after your father's accident."

She started to cry and I hugged her, holding her tight against me. "It's okay, Mom," I stroked her hair. "Did Dad die because he was protecting you?"

She took a deep breath, hitching on her words. "He did, but it was more than just me. He died trying to save the whole hospital, the patients included. I remember that awful day when gunmen came in the cover of darkness. They lined the patients up first and shot them execution style, then the witches came next." She shook while she continued to tell the story; the pain evident in her voice as she relived the tragedy. "They shot some of them also, but those were the lucky ones." She shook her head.

"The gunmen, led by my brothers, William and Thomas," her voice dripped with disgust when she said their names, "and their henchmen, assaulted several of the girls while the others still alive watched. Some were the children of the women. The men slit their throats and let them bleed out while they were being victimized." She hugged herself and I saw she was visibly shaking from the retelling of the brutality.

"Mom, I don't understand. Why didn't the witches use their powers against the men?"

She shook her head again, "They had surprise on their side."

I looked at her strangely, "wasn't someone there able to turn the pain on them like I do? I mean, I know my father did, but wasn't there anybody else?"

"No. Sam was the only one. Power like yours is rare and it wouldn't have mattered anyway because they were armed with an amulet. One made of dark magic, making whoever wore it impervious to a witch's power."

My eyes widened. "You mean there's a way to block our power?"

"Yes, apparently there is. My father procured it from somewhere in Europe and the whereabouts were secret even to him," she smiled.

"It took me a while to find that out. Mainly because of William's bragging about how he killed your father. He came to me while I was in the hospital and let me know all about it," she sneered her dissatisfaction. "The bastard told me he sucked him into an abyss he'll never come back from. I didn't know what he meant, but I'm sure it wasn't good because the man is pure acid, vile and disgusting, always spitting tobacco from where he keeps it tucked in his bottom lip." She shrugged, "I don't know what he meant, but I did notice one thing. When he came to see me, he was only wearing half of an amulet."

I looked at her curiously, "why do you think that was?"

"I have my theories. But I think it was broken in the fight with him and Sam, the thing is, I always wondered what happened to the other half. When your uncle came into the hospital wearing the amulet, it was whole." She looked at her hands with a contorted scowl on her face. "I'd love to have another crack at him. He's taken so much from me, and he should pay for his crimes," she sighed. "I do remember one thing about the amulet though," she raised her head, looking at me, "it had words written in Latin on it. I learned the language long ago in school and even though I'm not fluent, I could make out some of it." She cocked her head sideways, as her eyes probed upward, indicating she was deep in thought, "Cor divisum, it said. A heart divided."

I looked at her with curiosity, "what do you think it meant?"

"I don't know, but your father managed to get me and several others away from the main floor before the council's goon squad found us." Her face turned sad, as tears formed in her eyes and I could tell this part bothered her most. "If he hadn't, I fear I would've been among the first killed and probably tortured as well. I wanted him to stay with us, to escape and not go back, but he couldn't leave his patients and the other witches behind. He left to help them, and I never saw him again after that. The survivors were sent away, me included, and I didn't hear anymore about him until your uncle's visit. If he hadn't sacrificed himself for us, my brothers would have gotten to us first. Your father's intervention was the only thing that saved me."

I think about this, as my mind is filled with sadness at the loss of my father, but also the burden my mother has lived with all these years. The hate for my uncle's and my grandfather only heightened inside me, as my mother spilled the revelations of my family. "Oh, mom, he sounds like he was a good man, and I would've loved to meet him. Is there any way possible he could've survived?"

My mom shook her head "It's not likely. I think he would've contacted me by now. I think William may have been right and he's gone, never to be seen again. In that single night, the council wiped out or institutionalized nearly all the known witches in a thousand-mile radius. I was tucked away, becoming my father's dirty little secret. By that time, Matt was already born, and I was pregnant with you, Harper. Father had a nanny care for Matthew and you too soon after you were born, until I was well enough to care for you."

Anger boiled in me at the thought my family could do such a thing to their own people and it was more than I could stand. "Grandpa can't keep doing this. We need to do something," I protested.

She looked at me with tear filled eyes, as she snuffed, then sighed lightly. "There's nothing I can do, Harper. My father wanted me to live a normal life, so he tried to keep me from being a witch," she sighed. "He hadn't counted on me meeting Samuel and the rest of the witches we communed with." She stared into my eyes, looking wanly at me, "whatever you do, be careful not to show anyone, even your friends, and especially not your enemies. They'll find a way to expose you and then it'll be too late. If the council finds out you have the same powers as your father, or even suspect it, they'll find a way to kill you. I wish I'd told you this before you used your powers, but I saw no evidence of anything manifesting in you." Her eyes sparked. "I'll try to see if I can run interference at school. Please promise me you won't let anyone else know or won't show off or anything."

I smiled and took her hand. "Don't worry, mom, I won't," I started to stand, but sat back down. "Mom? Where is Matt? What institution?"

She wrung her hands, nervously cracking her fingers. "If I tell you, you can't go visit unless I'm with you, got it?"

I nodded.

"He's across town at the Hallstrom Institute, where he's been for years. It was the same place I was sent to after the massacre."

I patted her hand. "Okay. Thanks, Mom for being honest with me."

I stood and headed for the door, then opened it, but as I walked across the threshold, I looked over my shoulder at her. It looked like the weight of a thousand burdens rested on her shoulders, and after today's revelations, I'm sure they did.

***

At school I got some dirty looks from the kids. There were a few whispers, but nothing I couldn't handle. I saw Stacy and her friends were noticeably absent. I was happy they weren't there. I couldn't handle dealing with them. The entire day was uneventful, and I wasn't even called to the principal's office, as I expected I would be. It was as if the whole incident was forgotten about.

When I got home, I noticed my mother wasn't there. Strange, as she was usually home from work by this time. I figured maybe she went to see Matt. I wasn't sure, but secretly I was glad she wasn't there anyway. I wanted to do some research on what happened at the Salem Witch

Trials. I opened my mom's laptop on the table and began to search and what I found was grotesque. The regular history was there, but when I dug deeper, I found pictures of the torture devices used for interrogation. Witch cakes made with the urine of the accused and fed to their dogs to see if the animal would reveal them. Devices attached to either side of the legs and a wedge driven between them, causing the legs to bow and break. All to get the accused to say they were a witch and in league with the devil. There was a device called the Iron Maiden I was familiar with, as I'd seen it in several movies. It was usually used jokingly, but the real thing didn't look funny at all.

I closed the laptop and sat there nervously. I wanted to go see Matt, even though I knew mom wanted me to wait for her. But if she was already there, it wouldn't be a problem going, would it? I pulled out my phone and checked the location of the place on my GPS and found it was only a ten-minute bus ride. I checked my bag to make sure I had enough funds for the bus fare and saw my lunch money was in there. I rarely ate and mostly saved it for special emergencies.

I got on the bus and tried to find a place in the back where I wouldn't be disturbed. There were no seats available except in front by an old lady. The seat beside her was empty and once I sat there, I could see why. She had her arm in a sling, and I could only assume no one was around her because the chance of hurting her was too great. A thought came to mind. It was what my mom said about being healers and how we could do miraculous things to help people in that way. So, I asked her about her arm and how she hurt it.

She hung her head and answered with a mild voice. "I fell at home. A stupid accident. The doctors tell me there's an infection in there and I'll have to go to a home to get some nursing care with antibiotics and therapy, I suppose," she said, and I could see the tears welling in her eyes. "I prayed it would heal on its own if I took care of it, but I was wrong, I guess. I don't want to go to a home, but I'm all alone and I got no one to take care of my dog."

I could see real anguish there and her face showed desperation coming from the possibility of losing a long life of independence. The wrinkles around her eyes only made the look more poignant. She truly was hurting, mentally and emotionally, so I took my hands and placed them on her injured arm. She flinched, not sure if this was an insult or kind gesture. Her arm was cold, but I felt a heat beginning to generate and in seconds, my hands were searing, as though I'd touched a hot stove. She tried to pull away, but I wouldn't let her and the people beside us started shuffling from their seats, unsure if I intended to hurt the old woman. I held for a moment longer, then released her arm.

She relaxed, as did the people around us, and she looked at me strangely, then slowly removed her arm from the sling. She flexed her elbow, then extended it and her eyes widened.

"It doesn't hurt anymore. What'd you do?" she said. The puzzled look on her face was more like bewilderment.

I smiled. "Nothing. I gave you a gift is all."

A feeling of elation came over me and I knew what my mother meant. This felt much better than hurting someone. Stacy may have deserved her punishment, but something inside me changed when I hurt her and helping this lady seemed to, at least in part, fix it.

The lady left the bus smiling and I noticed the lines on her face were lessened and the worry gone, like she was a new person. I suppose I was too, and for the first time since discovering my powers, I was happy.

I got off the bus just outside the hospital and walked through the parking lot thankful to see my mom's car parked close to the front. I walked into the lobby and asked to see Matt Lansing. They directed me to the recreational room where my brother was sitting in a corner looking out the window. I hadn't seen him in so long and the thoughts of playing in the yard and the way he watched out for me; all came flooding back to my mind. He looked so lost sitting there, like he was looking for some dark angel to swoop down and fly him away. Maybe it was me.

I eased up to him and sat down. My stomach was a knot of emotions, wondering how he would react to me. He hadn't seen me in years, and he didn't look like himself. This wasn't my brother, only the former shell of him. "Hey, Matt," I said timidly.

He turned his head toward me, and I saw his face was slack, his expression flat. He had a small amount of drool on the edge of his mouth, as he looked at me up and down with the gaze of a curious child. "I wanted to come and see you sooner, but I didn't know where you were. Then mom finally told me you were here, so I came to visit. I saw her car outside and figured she'd be here too." Matt began to tremble, and his eyes widened with a look like a deer in the headlights. It was like he was afraid of me or something. "What's wrong, Matt? Did I say something to upset you?"

He turned to the window and rocked gently, mumbling to himself. Whatever Grandpa Silas did to him was unfathomable, and for the life of me, I couldn't understand why he was so bent on destroying his family. I suddenly wondered if it would be possible to heal Matt the same way I did with the woman on the bus? Without asking, I grabbed his arm and he instinctively tried to pull away, but just as before, I wouldn't let go. My hands heated up and I felt the energy flowing through him. His whole body shook violently, then I felt something. At first it was a prickly feeling like pins and needles through my skin, like some force was trying to prevent me from healing him. I concentrated harder until I felt something push back, as bolts of electricity ran up my arms. It hurt and I felt it creeping toward my head, then I heard a scream from somewhere in my mind. I let go, stumbling backward from the chair, falling on my bottom.

People were looking at me and an orderly came to give me assistance. He extended a hand, and I grabbed it, using him to stand up again.

"You okay, miss?" he said.

I nodded. "Yeah, just lost my balance for some reason. I guess my sugar must be low."

He looked at me thoughtfully. "Can I get you something to eat or drink?"

I shook my head. "No, I'll be fine. I've got a snack in my bag."

Satisfied, he turned to go back to the other side of the room.

I looked at Matt and saw his rocking was more pronounced. I think he knew all along what I was trying to do. For some strange reason, I think he was trying to keep me from helping him. I frowned and patted him on the hand. "Sorry, brother."

I turned to walk away, but I'd be back, I was sure of it. There had to be a way to bring him around. I started down the hall to the main door when I heard my mom's distressed voice in a room close by. I gazed down the hall and saw no one was there, just a long dark hallway, like something from several horror films I'd watched. There were multiple doors on either side with small windows near the top.

I slowly walked to the door where I heard her voice and eased my head up to see inside. She was there, tied to a table with leather straps around her wrists and ankles and a line hanging from a pole attached to her arm. I saw people in scrub outfits around her, one with a syringe. They injected something into the line, and I watched in horror as the liquid flowed through the tube and to the crease of my mom's elbow. She fought against the restraints, trying to break free, but her attempts were weak, as she looked depleted.

The scrubs turned for the door and I ducked into the adjoining hallway. I watched them as they walked to the area opposite where I was standing. The room was clear, so I ran in to see my mom and held her hand. She grabbed my hand, then raised her head as far from the table as she could. Her eyes were fading, and I knew she only had a moment to talk before whatever drugs they gave her started to take effect.

She spoke to me in a weak voice. "Harper? Why are you here?"

"Oh, mom, I came to see Matt. I saw your car in the parking lot and thought you'd be with him."

She breathed a shallow breath. "Take...take my purse over there," she pointed across the room, straining her hand against the restraint. "They haven't disposed of it yet. Go to the ATM in town and get as much as you can from my debit card. By the time..." she inhaled for more air and blinked, trying to hold her eyes open, "...they try to find you, you'll be long gone. Take my car and get out of town, but don't go to the bus station, they can track you there."

I nodded, unsure if this was a good idea, as I only recently learned to drive. "Are you sure? I only have my learner's permit."

She gave me a weak smile. "You can do it. You're strong, Harper, just like your father. Just be careful, take your time, drive slowly, and don't bring attention to yourself." She drew in a long breath. "Ditch the car as soon as you can, then run away and don't come back. Your grandpa's dangerous and will hurt you if he can, just like Matt and now me." Her breathing was becoming shallower and her voice labored, "he knows about you. I'm not sure if he knows you're like Samuel, but he knows. I'm sure the school told him, as he has spies everywhere." She struggled to get another breath, "either way, you must go." She let out a slow breath and head fell back against the table.

I reached for her, cradling my hand behind her head, then lifted it gently. "Mom? Mom? Please, don't leave me," I said, trying to elicit a response that didn't come. Tears fell from my eyes. I felt a lump in my throat and couldn't swallow, as I looked at her and shivered. Why was this happening? She didn't ask for it and now I was powerless to do anything. My world was falling apart. I only wanted to help her and Matt but I was left with nothing, only the regret of not being here sooner.

I heard people outside, coming my way. I had to leave, but didn't want to, I wanted to stay here with her, to protect my mom. To save her and my brother, but I realized this wasn't a possibility. I only had seconds to decide. My head was reeling. All the pressure I was under, threatened to drive me crazy. In the end, I had no other choice. I ran to the other side of the room and grabbed the purse, then eased the door open, peering around it to see if anyone was out there. I saw them, the scrubs were coming back, but they were far enough away they couldn't see me. I ran for the adjoining hallway, ducking into the darkness before I was detected.

My heart thudded in my chest. I'd never been more scared in my entire life, as I looked around and saw an exit sign at the end of the hall. I ran for it, but when I got there, I saw an emergency exit with a warning message. The alarm would sound if I pushed it open, but I didn't care. I only had seconds before they discovered the purse was missing and came looking for me, locking the place down before I could escape.

I slammed my hands against the door, pushing the long rectangular handle. It depressed and the door opened, then locked. I hadn't counted on the automatic lock kicking in. There was a small keypad by the door, but I didn't know the code. The alarm blared but I paid no attention to it and kept pushing on the door, turning, and leaning my body into it. I saw the scrubs running in my direction down the hall. I pushed against the door again and again, praying it would open. The scrubs were halfway to my location, when the door finally gave way, and I went tumbling backwards onto the pavement outside.

I slammed the door shut with my foot, just as the scrubs pushed on the door. It locked back in place, and I saw them in the small window looking at me. I saw them pushing the keypad but didn't wait for them to open the door. I turned and ran to the parking lot. I rounded the corner of the building and saw my mom's car, then heard shouting behind me. Hurried voices were trying to catch up to me, but I didn't give them a chance. I went to my mom's car and emptied the contents of her purse on the pavement by the driver's door. I fished through all the things and found the keys and her wallet. The rest I didn't need, so I jumped in and started the car. I put it in reverse and pushed the gas pedal, but the car lunged backward, running up on the grass. I hit the brake and my head violently snapped backward, then forward again. My extended arms on the steering wheel kept me from busting my face open.

I quickly buckled my seatbelt and saw the scrubs, along with a couple of security guards running with everything they had for me. I put the car in drive and pushed the gas pedal a little easier this time. I turned the steering wheel hard to one side and drove between the parked cars. One of the scrubs was faster than the others, and he jumped forward, hitting the fender of the car. I pushed the gas pedal down hard and it lurched forward, knocking him to the side. I continued to drive toward the exit, leaving him and the others behind.

I drove across town, realizing I'd have to ditch the car. I was sure they'd be looking for it and me. I found the bus station and dropped the car off there, but instead of getting a bus ticket, I started walking, figuring the abandoned car would throw them off my trail. That day

I vanished from the world I knew. I left my mom, my brother, my home, and everything I ever knew behind to become an afterthought. I vanished into the city and didn't look back, knowing my grandpa would look for me, I was sure of it, but he wouldn't find any trace of his granddaughter. I didn't forget about my mom and brother though. I'd have my revenge on my family one day, this I could be assured.

***

Six months have passed since the day I spoke to my mom. I've been living in New York, hiding among the countless people there, staying away from the old world of my New England town. I would've stayed away for good, but I saw some news one night come across the TV screen as I was eating dinner in a diner near my apartment. Billionaire philanthropist, Silas Lansing, passed away. The news wasn't shocking, the man was old after all, but it did get me thinking. Aside from my uncles, my mother would be his only living heir and if something were to happen to her brothers, she would inherit everything. I decided to leave right away. I know mom told me to never come back, but I owed it to her to get what she deserved. If I were to go into town under an assumed name, then leave before anyone knew who I was, I could achieve my goal. I could take out my uncles and get the fortune to my mom. I could live happily with my mom and brother. We'd never have to look over our shoulders again. The last part I knew to be wrong, as the other families my grandpa was connected to would never let it happen, but with enough money and control, it may not matter.

I was naïve to think he'd forgotten about me. Even in the grave, he had plans laid out to take care of any loose ends, me being one.

My grandpa may have been dead, but my uncles and cousins were still around.

I talked to Sally before I came back, and it took me a bit to convey to her I was using a different name. I finally identified myself and she let me know where the funeral was being held and all the arrangements. I would be at the funeral, but only as a spectator. My family couldn't know I was there. When the time was right, I'd confront my uncles and cousins. Hopefully, I'd have the element of surprise and they would have no clue about the power I possessed. I had it all planned out. I'd meet them at my grandpa's house and take them out one by one.

I failed to realize, in my grandpa's world, information was key, and connections ran deep in this old-world town. I tried to get in touch with Sally when I got to town, but she didn't answer my texts. I drove by her house, and it looked like no one was home and I didn't stop for fear I'd be detected.

I stopped for gas at a local convenience store and saw the one person I didn't need to run into. Stacy Bozeman. Of all the people I'd see when I came back, it would be her and I tried to leave before she caught up to me, but I was too late.

"Harper Lansing," she called out. Several heads turned in my direction, so I pulled the hood of my sweatshirt up in a vain attempt to hide, but I doubt it mattered. The Lansing name was well known, and the towns greatest benefactor had recently died. The name was on every tongue, I was sure. I saw her put a phone in her pocket and whoever she was talking to knew I was home. The thought dawned on me this was a bad idea, but it was too late now.

I turned to her, trying to make fleeting eye contact and saw her arm. It was in a brace, even after all these months. "Hey, Stacy, it's been a while."

She looked at me with disdain and I could feel the hate dripping from every fiber of her being. She had no need for chit chat and got straight to the point. "I don't know why you came back, but I suspect it has something to do with your grandpa's estate. Why you think your uncles will give you anything is beyond me," she started to turn away, but hesitated. "The little tricks you played at school won't help you here because they'll have you before the days out."

She turned for her car. She was right and my family was probably already looking for me. My time was short, I had to get to my uncles before they got to me.

I left Stacy with a small parting gift, as I got into my car. I cut myself on the right arm and heard her scream in pain, as I drove by using a one finger salute. My mind was lost thinking about the time not long ago, when I broke my arm to disfigure her. I was so caught up in the memory, I failed to see a car barreling from an alley, until it hit the front of mine. I had only a second to react, which wasn't nearly long enough as three armed men grabbed me from the vehicle before I could do anything. There were lots of people around, even a cop, but no one lifted a finger to help. My grandpa's influence ran deep here. In my mind I heard him laughing from somewhere distant and even though I barely knew the man; I felt his spirit was here. He was like a weight on my chest, heavy and ever present. I would feel his presence even more when his casket lay on me.

They drugged me and when I awoke, I found myself in a shallow grave beneath my grandpa. Thankfully, a small grouping of rocks propped the bottom of the casket, giving me room to move; not much though and I started to panic. I couldn't breathe, as the thought of being buried alive burned in my head. If I didn't get out of here, I'd be here forever, regenerating but never completely dying. A normal person would give up, accept their fate, and realize hope had abandoned them, but I was Harper Lansing. My father fought them, and he died trying. But I wouldn't, not here, and not today. I felt power coursing through me, as the heat in my veins seethed, giving me strength, I didn't know I possessed. I dug at the rocks and dirt around me, feeling the casket move above me. I had to be careful and move out from under the box before it pinned my leg. I managed to dig enough to give me room and the rest of my effort was spent burrowing up through the loose dirt.

By the time I got to the top, my arms were gashed and torn, and my breathing labored. I lay on my back, waiting for the burning in my lungs to subside and my wounds to heal. I'd inhaled dirt and mud and coughed, spitting the offending debris from my mouth. I rose to my hands and knees and let the chunks of mud fall from my hair. I heard thunder rolling on the horizon and saw the storm coming. Rain fell around me, and I welcomed it as it washed my face and eyes enough to see the fresh graves beside my grandpa's. Lightning illuminated the sky above me and I saw the names of Matthew and Julia Lansing, shining bright in gold trim on the small grave markers afforded to them. Rage burned through me. He wasn't content to hide them away this time but had them both killed.

The storm raged around me, as fresh torrents of rain fell, soaking me to the core. I looked at the headstone of Silas Lansing and laughed as I picked up a handful of dirt and smeared it across his name. "You think you had it all figured out, you old bastard. You'd silence the ones you didn't need. The only people who could stop you." I looked at the sky and cried, the rain mixing with my tears. A cold shiver fell across my body, as I raised a fist above my head. "Why? They only wanted to be left in peace!" I yelled out, as a large crash of thunder blasted through the air. The storm raged overhead, but it was only the beginning. There was a new storm coming, and my uncles would soon find out, this one couldn't be silenced.

***

Now I'm here, in my grandpa's house, facing the people who would have me destroyed. They surround me, all six of them. It wasn't easy getting in here. I had to go through a security guard and an electric fence; the voltage high enough to fry an elephant, or a security guard who came too close to investigate. I revel in their confused expressions. They look at me like I'm some zombie returned from dead. A piece of shit they thought wiped clean from their boots. My uncles, William and Thomas, and their four boys, Robert, Harold, Billy, and Lawrence. The last time I saw them, they were only children and we only had contact when we were in grade school. They went to a different high school than me. They're young but fully capable of fighting. Robert is the oldest, maybe eighteen by now, and probably full of anger, as I watch them grab weapons. I let them. Why not give them a false sense of security?

I saw the weaponry when I entered the house. There was a shotgun over the fireplace mantle and an axe and spears hanging on either side. The old house looks like a medieval castle from the outside and the inside is closely related with stone lining the walls and old brick inlays along the floors. I suppose the alarm system alerted them I was here. I wonder if they saw the dead guard outside, I stole the leather gloves from before I entered the house. I want to keep my fingerprints off everything.

I stand, bending my head to the side and my neck cracks like I'm older than my years. With all that's happened to me, I suppose I am and I'm sure I look disheveled, with my hair caked in mud. Like a wild thing from the forest.

The first to confront me is my uncle Thomas, holding the shotgun. He runs toward me screaming, expelling his distaste at my existence here. "I don't know how you did it, girl, but you shouldn't have come back here," he raises the gun. "Die, witch!"

The barrel of the gun is only inches from my head when I grab it and push it down, fire bursting from the end. It hits me hard, causing me to fall to my knees, grimacing. The pain is as intense as any I've ever felt. A fire burns in my middle as pieces of flesh are scattered on the floor in front of me, along with a copious amount of blood. The blast hit my midsection, taking a sideways trajectory, sheering off most of my hip. It's good because I don't know if I could heal from something so violent as a point blank blast from a shotgun and I don't intend to find out.

I look at my uncle and smile at his expression of surprise, but then I see the grimace of agony in his eyes as well. He grasps the middle of his body or what's left of it. The gaping hole where his pelvis and man parts used to be tells the story of why his pain is so great. I think I see—or maybe imagine—a piece of his penis lying in the scattered pulp on the floor. Either way, his emasculation is complete, and I'm satisfied with the kill. He falls forward in front of me, shaking, attempting to say something through his wet gurgles.

My wounds are nearly healed when I stand and turn to confront my next attacker. A cousin of mine. Thomas's son, Harold, I believe. He comes at me with the axe as I bring my arm up to shield my head. The axe goes through my hand, detaching it from the wrist with little resistance, landing in my clavicle with a low thunk. Blood sprayed from the wound, splashing him in the face while I revel in the excruciating pain, fueling my fever to kill them all.

I see the look of victory in his eyes. He thinks he's won, feeling he's beaten me, but he knows nothing of what I can do. He reaches for the handle, attempting to pull it free, then stops. His eyes are wide, as he turns his attention to his detached hand, writhing on the floor beside him. Blood gushes from his wrist and he shakes with the shock of what's happening, as he grabs for the wound but can't seem to get his arm to move. The open wound on his shoulder won't let him, as blood pours down the front of his chest. It looks deep and painful, as it spits like a geyser, sending torrents of crimson fluid into the air and onto his shaking body.

I grab the axe from my shoulder, gripping it with the healed hand—I'm amazed at how fast it regrew—and throw it on the floor in front of him, then he falls into me, convulsing with his face a startled mess of emotion.

"Go to sleep bitch," I say to him. The bile in my voice mixed with the satisfaction of my revenge kill. His eyes are wide with stunned disbelief as he lays there bleeding. I turn when I hear a swoosh in the air in front of me and I'm driven backwards from a spear in my abdomen. It goes through the small of my back and sticks me to the chair I stood from a moment ago.

I struggle to free myself as I glimpse Thomas's other son running toward me. My cousin Billy smiles, thinking he's ended me, but then grabs his chest. I see blood pouring from the hole there, as I reach for the spear and try to pull it free. I can't. It's stuck in the chair behind me. My cousin falls to his knees in front of me, but before he does, I grab his shoulders. Using him for leverage, I'm able to pull my body loose from the spear. I push him out of the way and fall forward to my knees as well, exhausted by the effort. I extend my arms in front of me and teeter on my hands and knees, trying to regain my composure. My body is healing, but the attacks, coming in rapid succession, are taking a toll. I managed to rise to my feet and look at the three of my family members, lying in fresh pools of blood and gore in front of me. The other three stand on the opposite side of the room and aren't as eager to engage.

My uncle William directs his sons to go to either side of the room, as they walk slowly along the side of the wall with my uncle taking the middle. *Are they trying to surround me?* The thought rolls through my clouded mind. If this is their plan of attack, it's clumsy, dangerous, and it'll never work. I shake the fog from my eyes and fight to regain my strength, as they inch ever closer.

I looked for a weapon and see the gun and axe are too far out of reach. So I turn to the spear behind me and grab it. I feel my cousins are close behind me. I manage to pull it free, just as Lawrence grabs my wrist. I don't have the room to hurl the spear, so I ram it into the top of my foot instead. It has the intended effect causing my cousin to howl with pain, as he releases me, falling backward to the floor, and grabbing for his foot.

I pull at the spear to free it before another attack comes, but I'm too late. My uncle William football tackles me, pushing me into the chairs behind and we both go crashing to the floor. I feel a chair hit my head, and my vision clouds, but I manage to stay conscious. He rolls sideways but doesn't seem affected by the head shot I took as he stands over me. It's then I notice the necklace he's wearing. It looks broken, like one half is missing. It has strange markings scribbled across it and I know it's the amulet my mom spoke of. It's more beautiful than I expected. It's bejeweled around the edges and is thicker and larger than I thought it would be. It's green like jade, almost translucent as the light reflects through it. I hadn't counted on my uncle being so clever and I realized then I'd miscalculated my advantage over him.

Before I can rise, my cousin Robert kicks me in the ribs. His boots are heavy, and I hear a snap on impact. He immediately kicks me again and I hear another crack. The sharp pain causes me to fall to the floor again, taking my breath. My lungs won't expand, and I feel a stitch in my side, radiating pain through my entire abdomen. I try to project the pain back on them, but neither is effected, and I see why. My cousin is wearing the other half of the amulet.

My uncle William crouches beside me and produces a knife from his belt. It's large with a wide blade, like something used for hunting to dress out the kill. The light from above reflects off the blade, shining in my eyes. He grabs my hair and pulls back hard, then brings the blade within an inch of my exposed neck, then turns his head to look at the carnage of his brother and nephews and laughs. His breath is vile. A foul odor emits from him when talks to me. It mixes with the smell of the tobacco stuffed in his bottom lip.

"The fools. I knew they'd go rushing in, not paying attention. They didn't know what their adversary was capable of," he shakes his head. "I knew all along what I was up against. But do you think I'd tell them?" He spits on my cheek. A wad of brown saliva drips along my face, making me crawl inside. It's like acid burning my skin. He smiles at me, slurping the spit left on his lip back in his mouth, then considers the knife. "You know, this is the same knife I tried to kill your father with," he laughs again, as spittle sprays from his mouth and onto my face, making me cringe. "In the end though it was this that did it," he says, raising the knife and pointing the tip toward the half of amulet around his neck. "It cracked but did the trick. I don't know what kind of magic it is, but your father didn't know what hit him."

He smiles, looking into my eyes. "Oh yeah, I forgot to tell you about your friend. Sally, was it?" My eyes grow wider with this statement, as my uncle clicks his tongue. "Oh, now, didn't know about that one?"

He laughs again, as loathsome bile from the words he speaks falls from his mouth, and I want to kill him before he says another word but can do nothing as he has the upper hand. "We had a good time with her. Me and your dead uncle over there," he nods his head in the direction of Thomas's limp body. "Oh, the way she screamed. I got a feeling it was her first time," he shakes his head. "She was still screaming when I opened her throat, gurgling blood and all. It was a shame I had to end it, 'cause I think she was starting to enjoy it." He raises his head and laughs again, until he coughs. Fresh spittle splatters my forehead, and it feels like a waterfall of sick vitriol.

"I guess while we're having this heart to heart, I'll tell you about your mom." He raises his eyebrows and turns his head slightly, grinning like some cat playing with its prey. "Julie was no fight at all. My dear sister was so drugged she couldn't do anything even if she wanted to. I just stepped up and slit her wrists. The same way I did your brother," he smiled wanly, like he was rehashing an old, but enjoyable memory. "Had to make it look like a suicide and all, because this was after the old man finally passed, mind you," he looked to the picture hanging on the wall of Silas. "He protected her and your brother and would've done the same for you if he was still around."

I feel his dirty fingers stuck in my hair, along with the blood of so many, Sally, my brother, and my mom. I take it in and feel anger rising inside me. My blood boils with the need to rip his head off. He redirects his gaze to me. "She wasn't a fighter, like you. I suppose once we take some of the fight out of you, you'll be better prepared to submit."

He pulls harder on my hair, and I produce a stifled scream. My midsection is still writhing and is now mixed with the pain to my scalp. It's agonizing, and I feel woozy like I'm going to pass out, but I won't. I've still got some fight in me, and the bastard won't violate me like he did my friend. He considers me, then slowly brings the knife to my neck, but I can't let it end this way. They can't win.

With the precision of a surgeon's hand, my uncle tediously places the thickest part of the blade against my neck as it penetrates slowly, methodically opening my tender flesh as he rocks it slowly side to side. I feel the stinging pain burn inside me, but I can't project it onto him. My cousin leans in to watch and his piece of the amulet swings haphazardly in the air, close to the other piece around my uncle's neck. I see the words on both pieces magically come to life when the two pieces are close. The words are familiar to me because they're in Latin. The classes I thought would never be of any use to me in school turned out to be helpful after all. *Cor divisum non protest quiescere.* A heart divided can never rest. It's the other half of the translation my mom came up with. But what did it mean?

The piece swings back away from the other and the words go away. A thought comes to my mind, as clear as if I were speaking. I'm being shown something. Is the amulet wanting to be whole? Maybe the pieces must join one another?

My uncle continues his drawn out cutting. He wants this to be painful and I know he wants me to suffer. I wonder if once he removes my head, I'll be dead. I doubt even a witch with my powers can survive a beheading. He won't do it though until he's had his way with me along with my cousins. They'll fuck me while I bleed out and then take off my head for good measure.

I must get the amulet from him, try to do as the enchanted piece wants me to. I stop struggling and instead welcome his advance. When he's close enough, I reach up and grab his neck and he instinctively pulls away, thrusting the knife deeper into my throat. I spit blood from my mouth and feel the liquid running down my throat, gagging me.

I feel nauseous as bile rises in my windpipe, mixing with the blood pouring down my chest. I gag as vomit erupts from my mouth.

My uncle momentarily pulls away, disgusted by this, but before he does, I dig my fingers into his neck, gaining purchase on the chain of the amulet. Once I have it securely, I pull with every ounce of energy I can muster. The chain snaps and the piece of amulet falls into the blood on the floor. My uncle releases me and scrambles for the necklace, struggling to find it in the pool of blood and vomit on the ground beneath me. "Robert, help me!" he yells.

My cousin is momentarily dumbfounded. I feel a sudden surge of power come over me that I'm able to direct toward my uncle. He stops and clutches his throat, as blood pours from the newly forming wound there, and I smile. I hear Robert scream to his brother, as I start to rise.

"Lawrence don't!" He warns him, but it's too late, as I feel the thrust of the spear through the middle of my back. The whispering sound of air escapes from the wound and I'm momentarily out of breath, as if my lung collapsed. Then suddenly, I can breathe again, as a burning sensation pours over me. I crane my neck to see Lawrence standing there, like he's exerting his dominance. I smile through my blood soaked teeth and spit a long stream of frothy pink liquid to the floor. I watch as it drips from my open mouth and laugh. *Fuck them, fuck them all. Motherfuckers thought they could stop me, but now we see who's hurting. Now, they'll feel my exquisite pain.* I watch as Lawrence falls to his knees in front of me, clutching his throat, trying to find his breath, as bubbles form in the blood pouring from his chest area. His face changes to a purple color and his eyes are wide with shock as he falls in front of me. His face plants in the river of blood flowing along the floor.

Robert tries to step by me, knowing he can do nothing for his brother and makes a move to help his father instead. I can do nothing, as I'm stuck to the floor with the spear and my hands and knees are propping me up. I decide to drop to the floor, letting the spear slide all the way through my body, feeling fresh pain, as the healing scar tissue rips open. I feel the air escaping my lungs again and the burning sensation is intense. But it only gives me more resolve to end them. With my free hands, I reached for his ankle and hold him tight.

"No, you don't," I say, and grab Robert's ankle, causing him to slide forward into the blood with his arms splayed in front of him. I see a knife strapped around his boot and I stretch my hand to retrieve it. My uncle is close by, clutching his neck as he attempts to stand. The wound wasn't deep enough to kill him, obviously. I'll have to remedy that soon. He has his back to Robert, oblivious to our struggle, as Robert tries to get to his feet again. Before he can, I move to the side, allowing my body weight to pull the spear loose from the floor. The pain is excruciating, and my breath leaves me again, then comes back. The loss of oxygen makes my head swim and dots blur my vision, but I won't pass out. I will not be denied my prize.

Robert turns to me with wide eyes while he watches me push the spear from my body. I must look crazed to him because my hair is stringy, caked with dirt and blood, and my clothes sodden with it. He scrambles forward on his hands and knees, but again, I won't let him. I jump on his back like a wild animal as I claw his neck, groping for the one thing I need to make me whole. The amulet is within my grasp, but he fights me, trying to keep me from retrieving it. I plunged the knife into his shoulder, screaming as I push his head into the blood. He cries out in pain as the blood from his wound sprays onto my face and I taste copper. It fills my senses, like I'm a warrior of old; a Viking bitch ready to kill. I snap the necklace from him and grab the piece of amulet. I roll Robert to the side and let him cower to the corner, grabbing his shoulder, and applying pressure to the wound.

"I found it," Uncle William cries out triumphantly, turning to me with a surprised look on his face. I flip my blood encrusted hair back and spit on him. Red tinged saliva spatters his face, making him wince, then step back slowly while holding the knife in front of him. He's visibly shaking even though he stands at least a foot taller.

Uncle William looks behind me and sees Lawrence, dead and lying in a massive pool of blood. Then he looks to Robert with the knife stuck in his shoulder as he tries to lick his wounds. My blood is mixed with theirs now. We're one big family and I see the anguish in his eyes at the loss in front of him. He looks to me like I'm the devil incarnate, as the fear in his eyes turns to rage.

"You think you've won, girl?" he holds his piece of the amulet in front of him, "but you can't do anything to me while I have this." His words are tinged with poison. I know he wants me dead, but I also see something else in his eyes, the look of desperation. His act of defiance is betrayed by it, and I have his mind reeling as his plans are unravelling right before him.

I smile and extend my arm in his direction, displaying the piece of the amulet I hold, using my fingers to manipulate it in his direction. His eyes study the piece and I see fresh worry there. "Not so smug now, are you?"

I leap for him, taking my piece of amulet and connecting with the one in his hand. He instinctively pushes the knife into my stomach, and I feel the blade sink to the hilt. It burns, but no more than any of the other weapons pushed on me tonight. I'm numb to it and I use the pain to fuel my anger toward him. I feel my hand burn where the two pieces meet. It feels wonderful, warming my heart, as it continues to glow brighter.

My uncle lets go of his piece, like it's a hot ember plucked from a fresh fire, one directed at him and his evil presence. The amulet melts into a greenish fluid, falling from my hand and onto the floor. William steps back, pulling the knife from my stomach, then pushes the weapon toward my neck. But his attack stopped mid stride. A man holds my uncle's arm at the wrist. An angelic figure, beautiful and glowing with brightness. I look at him curiously, as there's something familiar about him.

"Father?" I whisper, barely audible, more of a thought than an actual word.

He whirls my uncle William around to face him and my uncle stares at him in disbelief. His lips quiver, trying to form words, but the sound comes out as a raspy gurgle, "Samuel? But how?"

My father smiles at William as he holds on to both sides of his head. My father's hands squeeze and probe my uncle's skin causing tendrils of smoke to rise from where his fingers touch. William screams, reaching for my father's hands, but unable to free them from their grip on his head. I watch in utter amazement as the skin peels from his skull, revealing blood-soaked bone as the skin falls away. His eyes hover in their sockets, boiling like poached eggs. They shake furiously, then pop. The vitreous fluid runs down William's cheeks, combining with the blood to make a primordial soup running into his mouth and down onto his body. The smell of burning flesh permeates the air, stinging my nostrils, making me somewhat nauseous, but satisfyingly content. Like the smell of something warm from the kitchen you long for, but secretly wondering if it will be any good.

My Uncle's head sizzles and melts like a salted snail, until all is left is William's grinning black skull. Samuel smiles, releasing the body into the pooling blood below. Then my father turned his attention to my cousin. Robert is standing, shaking his head, slowly inching backward toward the wall. My father reaches into the mush of blood and gore left over from my vile family and retrieves my uncle's knife. He walks toward Robert and the young man starts to cry.

Robert extends his hands in front of him. "Please, no," he begs. "I'm not like him," he nods to the smoldering corpse of William. "He made me come here, made me do this. I had no choice."

His cries for mercy go on deaf ears. Mine and my father's. I don't feel sorry for him. He'd done his father's bidding, whether he had the taste for it or not. If they'd had their way, they'd be violating my bleeding body as we speak. He deserves no more mercy than my uncle did, and Samuel Petra seems to have no taste for it as he lowers the knife to my cousin's crotch. Robert bawls incessantly, clawing for purchase against the wall, but it offers no relief. His pain will be legendary, I know. His father's pain, I feel, is miniscule to what Robert will feel. My father sinks the knife deep into the young man's groin. I watch and see the look on Robert's face is a mix of pain and surprise as he screams loud enough to wake the dead. I look to the wall and think I see my grandpa's face contort from the excruciating utterance coming from my cousin's lips. I hope the motherfucker is hearing this from his grave.

The screams are replaced with gurgling while Samuel works the knife upward toward my cousin's chest. Tightly wrapped intestines spill from the newly opened chasm in Robert's midsection, and I see my cousin is still alive. His eyes wide open, as he shakes uncontrollably, staring down at his insides unwinding onto his feet. The smell of shit stings my nose as the inside of Robert's bowels seep onto the ground, mixing with his blood. He coughs, spitting frothy red from his mouth and splatters of crimson spittle hit my father's face. They turn to steam immediately when they touch his radiant skin; the glow like a seraphim angel too bright to see for fear of the eyes burning out.

Samuel Petra looks satisfied as he stops his thrust of the knife at chest level and gives it one more twist near the area of my cousin's heart before pulling it out again. My cousin's face stares forlornly at his butcher, and he spits fresh blood in response to the extraction of the instrument. Robert is half in this world and half out. No longer alive and vibrant, but more like a shell, soon to be impervious to the pain and frustrations his family has thrust on him all the years of his short life. I understand it fully and know he deserved his fate, but I can't help feeling some compassion for his plight.

My father raises the knife one more time, then thrusts the blade deep into the waning heart of Robert Lansing. The young man produces a barely audible gasp, then shutters and goes limp, falling to his knees, and planting face first into the river of blood and entrails at his feet.

My father turns to me and smiles, but says nothing, as his body begins to fade. He becomes a mist, dissipating to the ground and absorbed by something. I look to see the amulet, lying there, whole, and no longer broken. I wanted to talk to him and tell him about me and all the things I've been through. But I see it may be fruitless. I pick up the amulet and massage it with my fingers, feeling over the engraved inscription. I feel my father's presence there, bask in the glow of all the love of his last testament to me. The sacrifices he made to my mom and the people under his care, the blood he shed here was given to me in recompense for the slayings in the name of my grandfather's will. I feel if I have the amulet in my person, I'll always have his protection.

I look over the carnage and sigh. I suppose I'm my grandpa's last living heir, but I don't care though because I don't want his blood money. I want nothing to do with the Lansing family, as my mom and brother were all that mattered to me. I find the room the security cameras are kept in and destroy any evidence of me being there. I also found a safe in the room with a sizeable amount of money and I took it. Why not? Blood money or not, it will help me get away from here and disappear without being tracked. I checked to see if I left any footprints anywhere and see the river of blood shed here today covers any I made. The authorities would be hard pressed to find any evidence of me being here, but even if they do, I don't care. I'll be long gone before they find me.

Before I leave, I look at my grandfather's portrait. To me, he looks smug, even though his family—the ones who mattered to him any-way—have been simultaneously wiped out. I smiled, realizing I always had the power to stand up to him within me, but it had to be nurtured along. I take the knife my cousin was killed with and slash it across the face of my grandpa's portrait. A little parting gift and warning of sorts to those who will come to see the carnage here. The Lansing witches have won today, but there are others beyond my family on the Council of Hunters. The spirit of my mother and all that died before her, will live on through me. I leave here today, knowing they didn't die in vain, and soon, the rest of the Council will know too.

The End

Within Us

The Devil's Concubine

The clear glass of the visitation room glared in the overhead lighting, reflecting Katy's image back at her. It was much better than the one on the other side, as her brother, Lenny, sat there with the smile of an opossum eating shit and enjoying every morsel. Funny thing was those weren't even her words. Her daddy said it, even made it as clear as he could how Lenny was no count.

Lenny stared at her, then looked up and down, surveying the glass barrier. "They ain't taking any chances with you are they? I told you to behave and you'd be out faster," he shook his head, "you never was one to listen."

Katy wanted to rip his tongue out. Motherfucker still loved to taunt her, even though she hadn't seen him in six months. Funny how now, all of a sudden, he decides to show up. He should be apologizing, but instead, he's pulling his usual shit.

"You going back when you get out?" he said, licking his top teeth like he was filing them with his tongue. As sharp as his tongue was, he'd have them worn to nubs in no time.

"Don't know. Maybe I will. What's it to you?" Katy said. The disdain in her voice lay in the air like some heavy cloud. The weight of which could produce lightning.

Lenny laughed, as he leaned into the glass, blocking Katy's reflection and filling the area with his greasy presence. His shit eating grin was prominent enough to cover his face. "Well, the Devil take you then."

Katy stared at him and her expression was one of pure unadulterated hate for getting her here in the first place. Even after three years, her feeling about it hadn't changed. "Where else am I supposed to go, Lenny?" she looked to the countertop in front of her, then back to him, "you and daddy are the only kin I got. If it wasn't for your scheming, I wouldn't be here in the first place. You remember what you did?"

Lenny leaned back in his chair and started to speak, then stared over her head at the guard standing there. "This isn't the place. When you get out tomorrow, we'll talk more."

"All you do is talk, Lenny," Katy said, sneering at him, "Where is my daddy anyway? I haven't heard from him for a while." She thought about this. He used to call often, but she hadn't seen him in the past year. The only one she'd seen was Lenny. "Are you keeping him busy cleaning up your fuck ups?"

He leaned forward again, looking Katy directly in the eyes, "you can't go to daddy," he looked away, then back to her, "he's not well. You'll have to come with me first."

She considered him and what he was saying, thinking whatever Lenny was cooking up made her nervous, but if her daddy truly was sick, what choice did she have? She thought back on what Lenny had said six months ago, the last time he came in here. He had a wild look on his face and was spouting off something about the power that is within us. Katy had no idea what he was talking about. He acted like he was high, but she saw a genuine fear in his eyes. "You don't know what he's capable of, Katy," he said, referencing her daddy, "the man is bent on power and destruction."

She brushed it away, as Lenny never saw the favor of daddy like she did. She was sure he'd pushed daddy too far many times. That was then though, today, he was his usual smug self and Katy didn't like it. Something was off and she'd prefer to go on her own, finding a ride and go back to the house without him, but Katy had no idea what was going on in the real world. It was Lenny's place to manipulate any way he saw fit. "What do you mean, he's sick? What happened to him?"

Lenny sighed. "It's a long story and one I don't want to get into here. Tomorrow, when the bus drops you off, I'll be waiting for you, comprende?"

She shook her head and sighed, his bullshit would never end. "Okay but make sure you have Delilah with you," Katy smiled at the thought of her machete and the cold steel in her hand again.

Lenny laughed, "Delilah, huh? Trust me, that cunt will be waiting for you. She's stayed in the same place since you've been here," he smiled, showing a gold tooth that sparkled in the LED light above them. "Maybe once you two get back together, you can party again." He winked and Katy thought it strange he had a gold tooth like her daddy's. Was Lenny trying to emulate the man? Good luck.

Katy thought about Delilah, the machete her daddy gave to her on her sixteenth birthday. She remembered how he laughed and said he came up with the name after listening to an old song by some crooner named Tom Jones. When Katy asked what the song was about, he told her to listen to it sometime and it won't be hard to figure out. Katy did and asked no more questions.

The feel of the blade when she first held it gave her a sense of power she couldn't explain. It was perfectly balanced in every way and beautiful with a bone handle, polished to perfection and a shiny ruby at the base. There were small diamonds inlaid at the top of the handle, matching the sheen of the blade sharpened to perfection, and gleaming in the sunlight. Letters were inscribed on the side of the blade, and when Katy held it, she felt a surge go through her, a wanting. It was like some foreign entity took hold of her senses and not one she wanted to run from, but one she welcomed. Her daddy told her the blade originally came from somewhere in Mexico in the place her momma was born. It was magic, as it was touched by a Santería, making the machete course with power, channeling it to the one who held it.

He smiled wanly when he spoke about Delilah in his sultry Cajun accent harsh and gentle at the same time, "She only takes to a woman, as a woman gave her the magic in the first place," he laughed, "she is jealous that way too. You pick her up and you're not Katrina Sanchez anymore. You're just as it says on the blade. La concubina del diablo. The Devil's Concubine."

Katy stared at him, then read the inscription on Delilah, as the Spanish words stared back at her. At first, she had the limited understanding of an innocent child being groomed for something greater than herself. He looked into her wide eyes, as she soaked up his wisdom, and said, "Delilah. As I said, she's the devil's concubine," then gave a sinister laugh, "you wield her, and you will be too, Cher. To the devil, death is like sex. He's hard for it and will feed his mistress all that she wants."

What followed was years of practice with the blade, as she began to understand what he meant. When she held Delilah, she was someone else, a demon bent on destruction, as she learned of Delilah's taste for blood. She was thirsty and the blood of others, especially men who underestimated her, was the meal of choice.

Katy felt the urge to run instead of going with Lenny tomorrow, but the thought of Delilah slicing and dicing assholes did have a certain appeal. "Don't worry, I'll be there," she said.

Lenny stood from his chair and nodded to the guard standing behind him. He started to step towards the door and stopped, turning back toward Katy. "Remember, come see me first," he said, then turned for the door.

Katy stood and the guard reached for her hands, as she extended them, her wrists together. The guard clipped the restraints on her, then led her through the door. Later that evening, Katy lay on her bunk, as the thought of leaving her six-by-eight living quarters for the open air outside felt a bit unnerving, but she was ready. The thing that haunted her was what Lenny was up to, because the last time she trusted him, she ended up taking the rap for a crime he committed.

She thought about the night she was arrested. It was three years ago and not one day went by she didn't go over it in her head. She and Lenny were running their usual job and he was the point man, setting everything up, and she the kid sister running the go between. They mostly dealt in drug runs, carrying whatever the cartels were peddling at the time. Lenny always worked it out to take some off the top for himself, but Katy never messed with the stuff. Delilah gave her all the high she needed. Besides, she had to always stay sharp.

This time though, to her detriment, she'd become complacent, trusting Lenny too much. She thought she had drugs in the box she was taking to her client, but it was something else. An item Lenny forgot to mention, something neither of them were equipped to care for.

She remembered the day well, as the September sky was turquoise blue. The sun was high over the Mississippi Delta and in New Orleans, the humidity was low. Warm weather was making the run easier than usual, and Katy wore short sleeves and shorts. The uniform for a legitimate courier. In fact, she'd walked by Bobby, the cute UPS man who was always eyeing her on her routes, and he had the same get up. She remembered carrying the package up the stairs to apartment 5B. It was midway down the hall of the other units and Bobby was on the other end. He waved and she smiled at him.

Thoughts ran through her head of how sometimes she wanted to have a normal life, to settle down with someone like Bobby and have a few kids and get out of this batshit crazy life she led. No more danger and no watching over your shoulder to see if someone was there to do you harm. She'd have no reason to keep Delila at her side or the switchblade tucked in her sock. But Katy realized this was only a pipedream, as some people were designed to do certain things. It was their destiny.

She was given a key by Lenny and her instructions were to open the red door to the apartment, deposit the package inside, grab another waiting there, and leave. She would then take the other package to the actual destination of some warehouse on the east side of the city. What she hadn't counted on, what Lenny told her he hadn't counted on –she certainly didn't believe that shit–was the undercover cop waiting for her when she made it to the drop off spot.

The whole thing happened so fast, Katy barely had time to register. Lenny was supposed to be there to pick her up but wasn't. She was to drop the delivery van near the warehouse, go inside, deliver the package, then head out to the other side where Lenny was waiting. Only, there was a cop conveniently waiting for Katy. They had her cuffed and booked before she could spit out the word attorney. Lenny, of course, provided one. A piece of shit from downtown he probably paid off in drugs.

When he and Lenny came to the precinct to discuss Katy's plight, she knew she was fucked. He wore a corduroy jacket, the kind no self-respecting lawyer worth anything would wear, and it didn't fit him well either. He was a large man and the jacket looked old, like something he could've worn a while ago, but now it looked like some parasite trying to invade its host. His hair thinned on top, looking like fishing string coming from his scalp a strand at a time instead of in a grouping. He had beads of sweat on his forehead, either from being nervous or from the effort of packing his large pasty white frame around for any given amount of time. Either way, it didn't sit well with her.

He and Lenny sat down in the chairs across the table from her. The lawyer squeezed into his, looking uncomfortable, as his head turned side to side, staring down at the armrests on the chair, as if someone hadn't told him they would be there. He placed his briefcase on the table. It looked more like an attaché case, as it wasn't hard shelled but worn leather. He pulled some papers from inside and sat them on the table, then placed the case on the floor beside him. The lawyer then looked at Lenny, nodded, and turned his attention to Katy.

He cleared his throat. "Well then," he said, "this could've been a lot worse. This judge is fairly lenient on first time offenders," he shuffled in his seat, looking much more uncomfortable than he should, "your record's not horrible. I mean, there was the one case from juvenile court, but they rarely look at those." He shuffled the papers like he was doing something meaningful and not stalling. "I'm thinking if you plead guilty, we can get a decent plea deal without going to court."

Katy looked at the man incredulously, "Plea deal?" she furrowed her eyebrows at her brother, "the fuck is he talking about, Lenny?"

Lenny put his hands up in front of him, warding off the bad vibe rolling through the air in front of them, "this whole thing will probably be settled, and you can be walking from the jail with only probation," he smiled smugly, then shrugged, "no prison time at all."

Katy slammed her fist on the table and glared at Lenny, "what was I delivering? I want the truth, Lenny. I want to know why this time is different than the others? How could you let this happen?"

Lenny shook his head, "things go wrong sometimes. You know it was bound to happen sooner or later," he said nervously, "I mean, it could be me where you are just as easy.

She thought about the remorseful look on her brother's face that day, and realized it was more of Lenny's bullshit. He spoon fed it to her all the time, but gave her no other choice than to believe him. She went before the judge and found he wasn't lenient at all, as he gave her two and half years in prison with time served in jail, considering it was her first offense, meaning she'd be out about one month sooner. Maybe if her behavior was good—or so her sleazy lawyer told her—she'd be up for parole sooner. *Fucking, Lenny.* She thought about him often and what he'd done to make her life a living hell. The package turned out to be the usual shipment of fentanyl, but the other was the real item. Who knows what was in there and Katy doubted she'd ever find out either.

She talked to Lenny and her so called lawyer one more time before she went in and they told her about the fentanyl package but remained hushed about the other. "Don't worry about what was in the other," he'd said, "If they'd have caught you with it, you'd be facing a lot more prison time." She remembered feeling little consolation over the news. He added, "behave yourself in there and you'll be out a whole lot faster."

Her whole life was one of servitude with Lenny and her daddy, because she was raised that way. Kenneth Bergeron, the man she'd called daddy for as long as she could remember, started as a courier.

He worked his way up the corporate underground ladder, one bloody piece at a time. He was a man of means and he knew every trick and scheme on the planet, as he worked the streets growing up. Katy and her brother were both adopted by the man. He sought them out, looking for the abandoned children of homeless parents who were long forgotten by any family who once had connections to them. Her daddy knew what he was doing because he needed workers and had networks of kids but saw fit to elevate Katy and Lenny to the top for some reason.

He owned a renovated warehouse in Algiers Point across the river from the French Quarter. A little place off an alleyway nobody paid attention to. He'd turned it into living quarters on the upper floors, using the lower for a chop shop, where he had a team painting cars and running contraband. Shipments came in from vans or other vehicles brandishing one color and leaving as another. It was a fine operation, making her daddy a rich man.

He took an affinity to Katy when she first came to him as a scared little kid and because of this, wanted her to be able to take care of herself. It's why Delilah became her mistress. Because of his wealth he was able to afford the best martial arts trainer money could buy to teach Katy first how to defend herself, and then when she was older, the way of sword play. She remembered as an older teen, being unimpressed with the trainer he procured for her, and as a result, her efforts were listless. She was sixteen by then and her thoughts were on boys, friends (the few she had), and the desire to have a phone–something her daddy would have no part in. But Katy would soon learn, her daddy had no time for lazy girls and he took over the training himself. He personally put her through a hell much worse than any trainer could ever develop.

Katy reported to him early every day. She was home-schooled so her daddy controlled her school lessons, as well as her self-defense.

Katy learned how to balance Delilah, how to thrust and parry, ways to fall and make your opponent think they'd subdued you, then turning the tables on them and cutting low. The Achilles tendon was his area of choice and for good reason. Her daddy explained this is how you brought a tall opponent to your level. Once they were on the ground, you finished the kill. He would smile at her and say, "This is when the girl gets thirsty. When she wants to drink the blood of whoever is sacrificed to her. This is Delilah's alter of death, down here on the floor," he chuckled, "just make sure you cut 'em good enough they beg you for death, because dat's the only time Delilah will be satisfied."

Those times were magical for her, and Katy sought her daddy's approval, maybe because of a hidden longing for a parent's love, or maybe the pride of being the best killer she could be. Whatever the case, she would do anything her daddy said. Lenny was another story altogether. He loathed Kenneth Bergeron, even after all the man had done for him because, as Katy figured out, Lenny wanted the empire for himself, and he was biding his time. Katy thought maybe her daddy was sick like Lenny was telling her. It made sense, as Lenny was finally reaching for his opportunity. She wanted to see for herself and Katy would go see the man, ask him what he thought, and find out if her daddy's suspicions about Lenny were as strong as hers. Lenny lied to get her here, why wouldn't he lie about her daddy?

The lights went out above her, as it was time for everyone to settle down for the evening. Katy heard the murmurs around her. The sounds of the restless minds just doing their time and she was sure deals were going down, and sex being made, but she only had one thing on her mind. Getting out of here and going home. If Lenny had to take her, then so be it, and if Delilah was waiting for her like he said, then she may do some of the talking.

Katy stared at the concrete ceiling above her cell. She only had one more night of staring at the dark gray paint. She eyed a crack, extending from the corner to where the cell door anchored in the ceiling, then beyond, stretching the length of the cell. She'd traced it in her mind a thousand times. Many times, before, as she lay there on her bunk looking up, she imagined the crack was a river. One that let her drift to freedom. Tomorrow, she'll finally be on a raft out of here. Katy fell asleep not knowing what the next day would bring, but for once, she could care less.

The morning came and she was told to stay in her cell while her cellmate was directed toward the mess hall. The guard, Betsy Stahl, stood at attention outside. Stahl motioned for Katy to remain still while another guard checked the cell. After she'd done a thorough evaluation, she looked at Stahl and shook her head. Katy knew what they were up to. They wanted to make sure she didn't leave anything behind for her cellmate to use. No drug contraband to be exact. But Katy knew better, as she was too close to release to fuck it up now.

She didn't want any trouble with the guards anyway, remembering the last time it happened she ended up in solitary and got her sentence extended. The big guard shoved her face into the wall, blaming Katy for an insurrection that was clearly not her fault. When Katy first came to Louisiana Correctional Institute for Women—LCIW for short—she was thrust into a life of hell. The place was overcrowded and understaffed, so things got by the watchful eye of the guards. She was trying to be good and live by the rules, staying out of fights, so she could get out early. She was rewarded by becoming someone's bitch.

Greta Tunny stood six-one and looked out of place by other women's standards. When Katy first saw the androgynous woman, she thought at first, she might have a dick. Greta's fingers alone were larger than some cocks Katy had ridden. They were meaty round things and not at all gentle. Katy had been with a few other women before Greta—she usually preferred women. They were all Mother Theresa compared to her. To make things worse, Greta was her bunkmate and the first time the lights went out, Katy felt the woman fondling her in the dark. She cupped Katy's tits first, then eased her hand between her legs. When Katy protested, Greta pulled her from the top bunk, forcing Katy into her crotch. Greta's pants were already off and she held Katy on both sides of the head, rubbing Katy's face in her vagina. She inhaled the scent of Greta, whether she wanted to or not. To make things worse, Greta produced a lot of discharge, more than Katy was used to, and at this vantage point, it was hard to avoid. Katy's face was covered.

This made her angry and she wanted nothing more than to bite into Greta and make her stop. She had no recourse though, as Greta was incredibly strong and more than a match for Katy's five-foot-four frame. If she had Delilah with her, it'd be a different story entirely.

Greta massaged the back of Katy's head. "You better start licking, little dove." the name she gave Katy that night. Katy tried to pull away, get a breath for a second, but felt something scratch the side of her head. She understood quickly, Greta meant business, as the woman held some kind of crude shank and she had it poised to puncture Katy's skull if she disobeyed. So, Katy did as she was told. She tried to recall what it was like to enjoy this. When she was a willing participant. It was sweet and gentle, a time to get in touch with her inner woman. It helped a little, but not much.

She licked Greta's clitoris, teasing it the way she'd done with the others, until she heard the woman coo. "Now, we're talking. You pretty good. I had a feeling that little tongue of yours could find the spot," she said, as she massaged Katy's head. She licked the length of Greta's opening a few times, then settled on her clitoris, sucking gently. Greta's labia folds were thicker than Katy was used to, making it harder to find the button in the center. She probed deeper with her tongue until she found what she was looking for. The sweet inner layer of the tootsie pop. She used her tongue to apply pressure to the button, while simultaneously massaging the labia with her lips and teeth. Not biting–oh she wanted to–but giving it care. She took two fingers and gently pressed them into her opening, moving in and out rhythmically. Greta moaned, gripping Katy's head tighter, then bucked her hips, pushing them into Katy. She cried out, stifling a full-on scream.

Greta shuddered then released Katy's head, as her juices washed into Katy's mouth. "Oh, little dove. I've had a few white girls in my time, but I think you must be the best."

Katy wasn't white, but Latino. Greta didn't seem to care, as she shoved Katy to the floor, causing her to flop on her butt, humiliated, but glad to be done with this shit. She leaped for the water fountain above the toilet, but Greta scolded her. "Get on up to your bunk before I change my mind and shank your ass."

Katy did as she was told, as she was a subservient dog, listening to her master and afraid to get the switch. She lay there in the dark, staring at nothing, feeling her insides were drained with the taste of Greta's cum in her mouth. She wiped her tongue with her hand but couldn't rid her tastebuds of the saltiness. All she could think of was getting out of this fucking place and finding Lenny, then take her machete to his fucking head. Too bad she didn't have her girl here. But Katy knew this kind of thinking would get her nowhere and if the worst she had to do was endure Greta's occasional bush munch, she could do it, no matter how disgusting it made her feel. *Be good and get out quickly.* The thought rolled in her mind with little effort.

The days fell into weeks. She'd been in the cell with Greta a month now and things were going well. Greta even protected her in the yard, making sure nobody else was going to get a piece of her little dove with the magic tongue. Katy even endured Greta's meaty fingers and faked orgasms when Greta would work them in and out of her. The one thing Greta wouldn't do—Katy was grateful for it—was bury her face in Katy's midsection. The fingers were bad enough, but they had a forcefulness to them that the tongue didn't. Tongues were more intimate. Katy wanted no part of knowing Greta that way, as it was bad enough that she was forced to lick Greta into submission. She only wanted to do what she had to do and be left alone, then get out and back to reality in a few months. Her only hope was she and Greta would be separated. But then, who knew who her next cellmate would be. They had to be better than Greta. Katy only had to mind her place and behave and this would all be over soon enough.

The second month though, things took a turn for the worse. It was one night, as she and Greta returned from the shower; a normal part of their daily routine. This time was different though and Greta was pissed. Katy had done nothing to make her mad, only smiled at another girl and asked for soap. The girl obliged but stopped and stared at the tattoo on Katy's arm. The girl, Latino like Katy, studied it for a moment, then looked at her, "the Devil's concubine?" she asked, "is that what it says?"

Katy nodded. Her daddy took her to get it not long after she started her training with Delilah and it was a symbol of pride for Katy. She went about her business, even sharing the soap with Greta. When they got back to the cell and the lights were out, Greta pulled Katy from the top bunk and splayed her across the bottom one.

"You don't be looking at no other pussy, bitch. You're mine, you get it?" Greta scolded.

Katy tried to fight her off, but it was impossible. Greta was too damned strong to wrestle with and Katy quickly found herself on the losing end. The big woman jerked Katy's pants off, ripping the seam at the top. She stuck her finger to the hilt of Katy's tender vagina.

The act was painful, as a burning seared through her, and the tender skin around her vaginal opening tore loose. Something wet poured from her insides and she imagined her blood was staining the sheets below. Katy wasn't aroused by this display of brutality, but Greta smiled, seeming to enjoy it. She spat on Katy's pussy and rubbed it with her free hand, using the added moisture to push in farther. Katy stifled a scream, but didn't want to cry out, giving the beast the satisfaction of breaking her. Katy had no choice but to endure the pain of the assault and she bit her lip hard to subvert the hurt somewhere else.

Take it you dog, let it go, this will all be over soon, and you can go home. Home to Delilah and her musings of death. How she wished she had the blade in her hand, as the urge to slice Greta's head clean without any effort surged inside her. But she did nothing, only let the beast have her way, taking it in, holding it deep inside where she could use it later.

Greta paused for a moment, pulling her fingers from Katy, but she did nothing, only lay there hoping Greta was done. The woman hovered over her, breathing heavily from the exertion of her efforts. Katy saw Greta's silhouette in the darkness and watched as she sniffed her hands, like a predator savoring the fresh blood of its prey. Katy heard a maniacal laugh come from the woman, like something had snapped. Greta's next thrust at Katy came violently, instead of using her fingers on Katy's throbbing womanhood, she used her fist. Katy bit harder on her lips, as this assault was much worse, sending hot shudders of pain coursing through her body. This was too much and

Katy felt something inside snap. A hollow, empty calling came from deep within and it burrowed its way out and wouldn't be denied. Katy screamed as loud as she could and she didn't care if it brought the guards. She'd had enough. Enough of the humiliation and enough of being everyone's scapegoat. If she was supposed to be the dog then so be it, but everyone better stand back, because this dog has been backed into a corner. You know what happens when a wounded animal can't find a way out? It strikes back.

Katy rolled herself to the side, taking the next blow of Greta's fist in her ribs. She felt a sharp stab of pain go through her, but didn't care, it was miniscule to what she was enduring. Katy rolled onto her back again, and with her legs cocked, thrust all the power she could muster into Greta's midsection. The beast let out a gush of air, like a balloon being released. She fell from the bunk and onto the floor, rolling backward into the cell door, hitting the metal bars with her head. Katy wasn't done though and she jumped from the bunk like some crazed wolf. She landed on Greta, straddling her legs across the woman's lap. Katy pummeled Greta's face, first with her fists, then with her elbows. The way her daddy taught her.

She remembered what he said, *"you want to hurt someone, then do it. Take them out of commission, use the elbow because it's more akin to a knife. They will cut the face of your opponent and make them submit much faster."* It had the desired effect, as Katy's elbows were sharp and defined from all her years working out. Sharp like Delilah's edge. Katy mused over her machete while hitting Greta again and again. The woman gave nothing back, because she had nothing to give, but Katy had a lot saved up for her. The lights suddenly flashed on, and Katy could hear footsteps shuffling up the corridor outside the cell. She paid no attention to them and wouldn't be deterred from the task at hand.

This was personal and she'd make damn sure to get her fill of what she wanted.

She renewed her attack, smiling at the amount of blood pouring from Greta's face. She felt the snap of bone, as she brought her elbow down violently against Greta. The woman was unresponsive, but Katy kept at it, her work wasn't done. She needed to kill this asshole and make her feel the same pain Katy did, but much worse.

The door to the cell opened and Katy and Greta tumbled into the corridor. Katy didn't stop hitting her and kept the assault going. There was no end to the pain inside her and no end to the punishment she intended to unleash. She heard the muffled cries of the guards somewhere in the back of her mind, but they were in a different universe. One that existed somewhere in the normal world. Katy's world was destruction and pain on an unimaginable level. She was pulled from it when she felt herself being hoisted into the air.

Betsy Stahl and another guard pushed Katy to the back of the cell and Stahl slammed her against the wall, smashing her nose, causing it to gush blood. Katy remembered the feeling of the burning sting way inside her nasal cavity, as her sinuses filled with blood. Both guards grabbed her and threw her belly first onto the bunk, as they attempted to restrain her. The guards outweighed her by at least fifty pounds apiece, but they had nothing on her fury. It was a high-pressure cyclone, wrecking anything in its path. She fought them, thrashing her legs, catching one guard in the stomach, and doubling her over. By the time the fight was done, both Katy's legs and arms were tied down.

She saw Greta's limp body lying on the floor, as she was being carried from the cell. Katy was pleased. Blood pooled around her head and Greta's face was like uncooked hamburger, not clean, but raw and bloody. Pieces of flesh lay flayed from around her nose and her face was swollen and engorged with brackish pools of black fluid streaming from every orifice. More guards had shown up, and checked Greta's breathing, then turned her over. Blood poured in coughing bursts from her mouth and Katy heard a wheezing sound, like a tire deflating coming from Greta's mouth. She'd probably live, but that wasn't Katy's desire. A little more time is all she needed to end Greta for good. Too bad she was denied.

Betsy and the other guard picked Katy up to where her feet weren't touching the ground. She hovered there like some avenging angel bent on the destruction of the world. All Katy could see was blood and fire. It was the way of Delilah and she wished for her ill bent mistress to be by her side. If only for a second to deliver death on a scale unimaginable.

Katy spent the next month in a holding cell, all alone, but she welcomed the isolation and breathed in the desperation of her state. When she was left to sit in the darkness, to think about things, all she could concentrate on was Delilah. She would be out of this hell someday and back by her side. The elation of holding her blade again and using her to bring pain on the insurrectionists who plotted their demise would be epic. She found herself smiling at the thought and it was all she needed to get by.

When Katy was released back to the regular population, she seemed to earn new respect amongst her peers. Word of the beating she gave Greta circulated quickly. It was the ferocity of the attack talked about most and the sheer brutality. It was like some switch flipped on in Katy. There had been fights before but never one requiring the amount of reconstructive surgery Greta needed, as part of the woman's face caved in. Katy smiled when she heard this, because she did as her daddy taught her. *If you're going to do it, then make damn sure you do it right.* The words resonated in her mind and nestled in among the aisles of pain. Rote memory of how to doll out punishment. She felt her daddy was close by when she beat Greta and felt his presence there, and only there. Once the fight was done, he left her and he never showed up in the holding cell or when she was back in regular population. Only Lenny did.

For her insurrection, the parole board tacked on another six months to her sentence. It added additional misery, but at least she didn't have to worry about serving anyone. She only had to do her time. She remembered fondly the way she thought afterwards. *Fuck all of them. I'm doing my thing now. Ain't nobody controlling me anymore.*

Those things were behind her now, and she'd never be anyone's bitch again. Not even Lenny's. Katy extended her hands for Stahl to place the restraints on them and the big guard pulled them tight against Katy's skin. Stahl smiled, then gave them another pull for good measure. Katy winced but never made a sound, as she stared at the woman, giving her a look that would melt the skin off most people. But Betsy Stahl didn't seem bothered by it and kept the same affect no matter the intimidation factor.

Betsy stepped beside Katy, then waited for the other guard to take her place on the other side. They pushed her forward, shoving her toward the entrance. Katy had a vision of what this day would be like, figuring there would be prisoners jeering and giving her shit as she walked out the door. But the corridor was silent, as they were all in the cafeteria, eating breakfast while she was led away. She was taken to a room with a guard behind a wall. They had a box with whatever belongings Katy had when she entered LCIW. The guard helping Betsy stepped in front of her and produced a key to remove the restraints. Betsy reached for the box and laid it on top of Katy's outstretched arms.

"You can go in there to change," Betsy motioned to a small bathroom beside the desk. Katy walked slowly toward it and opened the door then closed it behind her. She was surprised when no one came in with her. It was the first time since she got here no one was watching her undress. The indignity of others staring at all your private parts was something you never got used to. When other guards and some inmates copped a feel of your breasts or ass, it was hard to let that shit go. Even after the fight with Greta, it happened, although not as often. When she got out, if someone dared do something along those lines, there'd be hell to pay.

She pulled her jeans on, amazed they still fit, but they were a bit looser than before. She'd lost weight, even though she worked out whenever she could, as there was little else to do. She stepped from the bathroom and gathered the rest of her belongings. A T-shirt and a phone that no longer worked. A brush and a couple of hair ties. She placed them in the old leather backpack she brought with her three years ago, then hoisted the bag on her shoulder and stepped in front of Stahl.

Betsy smiled at her. "Be seeing you again soon." The big guard smirked, then nodded for the locked door at the end of the corridor.

Katy smiled back at her and was happy to get at least a little rise out of the serious woman. "Not in this lifetime," she said, then headed for the door.

Betsy produced a card and placed it on the black panel next to the door. A loud alarm sounded, and the door came free. The wind rushed in, and Katy could smell the breeze outside. She'd been in the courtyard many times before and felt the air on her face, and it was nice, but the air outside the prison walls had a different feeling, a smell all its own. The time of year wasn't lost on her either. September was the month she was busted and many memories rushed past her mind, but she pushed them away and concentrated instead on her journey out of here.

The walkway to the gate was long, like a gray river with no end. It seemed surreal she was leaving this place for good and going back to the real world for the first time in so long. She wondered if the world had changed. She supposed some things had, but the business would still be there and Lenny would be setting up more jobs for her. That much she could be assured.

The metal gate clacked loudly, as it slid open to allow Katy to walk outside the prison grounds. A bus with LCIW printed in large black letters on the side waited for her and Betsy Stahl, stiff and unyielding to the end, walked Katy toward it. The side door opened, and Katy stepped inside and shuffled her way down the aisle, sitting on the side facing the prison. She stared out the window and the bus began to move, as uneasy thoughts invaded her mind. Leaving the prison was what she wanted, but going back to Lenny made her feel queasy. The uneasiness gave her pause, as the man was a schemer and she had to be on guard against him.

Thirty minutes later, the bus pulled into a small station. Katy scanned the parking lot and saw Lenny sitting on the hood of a black Chrysler, smoking a cigarette while looking at his phone. He was smoking again. She noticed. He said he'd given them up a long time ago, but apparently, he didn't stick with it.

Katy stepped from the bus and put her feet on the pavement. It felt different than the concrete she stood on for the past three years for reasons she couldn't explain, but it was similar to the difference in the air quality. She hoisted her bag onto her shoulder and headed toward the car. Lenny looked up from his phone and jumped from the hood, then stepped toward the back door. A light breeze blew past him, but his hair didn't budge. He had so much paste in it, it had no chance to move. He opened the door for her and Katy threw her backpack in, then stepped into the car, ducking her head to clear the top. Lenny loved low sitting cars, and black, they always had to be black.

Katy saw a man sitting in the passenger seat. He was large and wore an ill fitting suit and his neck was thick, like a tree trunk from the base of his head down to his shoulders. Veins bulged on the sides and beads of sweat formed on his forehead. He had a nervous shake, like he was perpetually always on guard, ready for the first sign of danger. Katy wondered where Lenny found these people.

She scanned the backseat but didn't see Delilah anywhere and concern covered her face.

"You looking for this," Lenny said. He tossed the machete back at her and Katy caught Delilah, pulling her close. "You'll want this too," he said and tossed back a switchblade knife. It was the one she kept tucked in her sock for backup. She sat it to the side and studied the leather casing Delilah was sheathed in, then smiled. The smell of the worn leather was as sweet as ever. The strap used to secure the case to her body, hung limply off the back of the sheath ready to be cinched comfortably on her back. She pulled Delilah from her nest and held the blade in front of her face. She looked at her reflection in the polished metal and read the words inscribed there written in the same Spanish words on her forearm. *La concubina del diablo, the Devil's Concubine.* Katy cherished it and felt the urge to cut someone or something. She looked at Lenny and saw he was turned toward the steering wheel, reaching for the ignition. Katy thrust Delilah forward, placing her within a centimeter of Lenny's neck.

The large man instinctively reached into his jacket and pulled a gun halfway out. Lenny extended a hand to him, gesturing for him to put it away. "It's okay, Lou. She won't hurt me."

The gorilla of a man eased the gun back into its holster under his coat, but the distaste for this idea showed on his face.

Lenny turned slowly toward Katy, careful not to push his luck, or his neck, on Delilah or the girl wielding her. "What the fuck you doing, little sister?" He said.

Katy pushed the blade closer to her brother's throat and he grimaced. "Take me to Daddy, now you motherfucker!"

The big man fidgeted in his seat. He looked like he wanted to reach for his gun again but wasn't sure if he should, as more sweat formed on his head and the man looked like he'd spontaneously combust at any minute.

Lenny put his hands up in a truce gesture. "Who said I wasn't?"

Katy eased up a little but kept Delilah close to Lenny's neck. "Yesterday you told me not to go there alone and now I want to know why," she said, then applied slight pressure to his carotid artery. Enough to put a small scratch on the skin. Thoughts rolled through her mind. *How easy it'd be to slide the thirsty girl across his throat. Delilah would fuck him up good, then she'd lap that blood up like eating pussy. Just what my girl needs.*

"Ease the fuck up, Katy," Lenny said, "do I have to remind you who has the gun?" His eyes rolled to Lou, who had his hand inside his coat, ready for the order from Lenny.

Katy pulled the blade away from Lenny's neck. He grabbed a napkin from inside his coat and dabbed the area around his neck. He looked at her, frowning his displeasure at the cut she left there.

"Listen, I know it's been a while since you held the bitch, but don't be getting paranoid on me," he sighed and looked at the big man, "Lou?" Lenny gestured with his head toward the door.

Lou said nothing, only opened the car door and stepped out, then closed it behind him. Katy watched him pull out a cigarette, light it, and walk away from the car, casually making his way across the parking lot.

Lenny watched too, while he pulled a pack of cigarettes from his shirt pocket, then turned to Katy. "What I'm about to tell you can't be repeated. You get me?"

Katy placed Delilah in her sheath and eased into the plush leather seat of the Chrysler. "I'm listening," she said smugly.

Lenny shook his head, "The old man isn't doing too good. He's been holed up in his bedroom for the last few months." he pulled a cigarette from the pack and put it in his mouth. He tipped the pack toward Katy, but she refused. He laughed, "I forgot, you stopped smoking."

Katy protested. "Yeah, just like you did? Besides, I never started. Remember asshole? I don't count you blowing it in my face."

Lenny shrugged, "Fair enough." He lit the cigarette and took a deep draw and blew the smoke from his mouth, paying little attention to whether it bothered her or not. "Listen. At first, I didn't want you going over there, picking up on the past, because I want better for you, sis. I want you to be something big in this organization. The old man ain't going to be around much longer, you know?"

Katy looked out the window. This faux concern he was throwing at her only enforced his weak stature, as he was a slimeball to the core, and Katy did not trust him. "That's funny, he was fine when I went in. What happened?"

"He's old, girl. What do you think happened? If you'd listen to reason occasionally, instead of thinking you got to beat your way through life, you might get an understanding of the way things work." Lenny said, shaking his head, in a show of disgust.

She turned to him, giving him a blank stare. Katy thought about the way she handled Greta at first in a vain attempt to make things easier for herself and she also thought about the way the whole thing ended. Releasing the animal inside her may not win any mercy from a parole board, but it gave her respect among her peers. It was just like her daddy taught her, you take no shit and take no prisoners.

Lenny took another long drag, then looked at the seat beside him, like Katy was there instead of in the back. He was nervous, she could see, as his fingers shook slightly. The ashes from the cigarette fell to the seat and he wiped it off before the fire burned a hole there, then he let out a slow steady breath. "We got to go see the old man. He's been asking for you."

Katy's eyes widened. "I thought you said he was sick?"

Lenny turned his head toward the steering wheel. "He is, but he can still talk. At least for now." Lenny opened the door and stepped outside, then reached inside the car and pushed the middle of the steering wheel. The car horn bleated and Lou looked up from the bench he was sitting on. Lenny motioned for him.

Katy looked out the window to where the big man sat and saw a small child was beside him. The scene was ridiculously out of place. The behemoth of a man, sitting next to the innocent child. The only thing needed was for the child to produce a toy for Frankenstein to cuddle. *It's a good thing there's nobody around with pitchforks and torches.* She thought.

Lou came sauntering toward the car, then opened the passenger door to get in. The car leaned to the side for a moment before righting itself. Lenny got in and turned the ignition key and Katy felt the low rumble of the engine. She could tell Lenny had been working on it, as he was never satisfied with factory specs. As they drove, she thought about her daddy. Kenneth Bergeron was tough but gentle in his own way. She'd been taught to fight at an early age, but he also wanted her to engage in reading. To gather as much information as possible about the world and its workings. He was into occult type things. Mostly voodoo he'd picked up in the deepest, darkest parts of New Orleans.

The places closed to tourists. He used more than chicken feet and animal sacrifices, but that stuff was prominent on his table. Various powders and books with symbols and rituals she never understood lay strewn together in his workspace as well. Daddy would burn candles and incense in his library while they studied books. Those were good times and the things a girl who adored her mentor remembers. Katy wondered if Lenny was ever part of that world, but she doubted it. Daddy was particular about who he let in and rarely did anyone else grace the door while they were in the library. Maybe the occasional courier to let him know a delivery had arrived, but overall he seemed to have an affinity for giving Katy all his attention. It was something she never forgot.

She remembered the light chanting he would do, as she watched him across the table. His face glowed in the dim candlelight and the smoke covered his head, encompassing him in an ethereal presence. Like he was somewhere else in another world entirely. It spooked her back then, but as she got older, she toughened to his ways. Katy remembered the childlike innocence of her daddy while he was conjuring and the way he laughed, like a child playing with fire, never realizing they could get burned. She secretly wondered if this is why he was sick.

The last time Katy witnessed his use of rituals, she was nineteen and Lenny was pulling her away for jobs, leaving little time to spend with her daddy. Lenny told her the old man wanted her on the streets, keeping the customers happy and secretly, she wanted out of the building. She was ready to go where the action was, where she and Delilah could be of best use, but her daddy wouldn't allow it until he thought she was ready. Katy discussed this with him, and he daddy finally gave her his blessing, but not before he bestowed some wisdom on her.

She never forgot what he said, "you and Delilah are one in the same. It's in your blood, Cher," he spoke in his matter of fact way, like you should already know these things, "feel her, soak her in, then you'll understand her true power. Dat's when the user become the used."

Those words never became truer until she found herself face to face with impossible odds on her and Lenny's first run across the border. Everything went to shit when the Trio de le Meutre gang showed up. The name loosely translated meant the trio of death. Three cartel members who rose to power by brutally slaughtering any competition in the state of Nuevo Leon, Mexico. Lenny and Katy were delivering to a rival of the trio, a gang with some nondescript name no different than their clothing and demeanor, but they paid better. The plan was to go in after dark, meet in a large airplane hangar, make the deal, and get the fuck out of there before anyone suspected what was going down. It didn't go as planned, but then, did anything Lenny put together go as planned?

Katy didn't care, but was actually happy, because it gave her an opportunity to use Delilah. Those fuckers had no idea what they were up against and when they burst in with their large Cadillac Escalades, Lenny pulled his gun, along with the rest of the rival cartel members in the room. Katy walked forward into the middle of the large hangar, holding Delilah by her side.

Lenny spoke up, "Katy? The fuck you doing?" he protested, "get back here!"

She heard him tell his men to keep their guns down and not to shoot. No one from the trio fired a shot at first, they only stared at the boldness of this chica. One of the members stood from where he was crouched beside the SUV, smugly, like he had no fear, then his eyes widened when he read the tattoo on Katy's arm. Katy was ready to rain hell upon them, but gave him a minute to let it sink in.

He spoke loudly to the others, voicing his warning of what they were up against. "La concubina del diablo," he cried. She smiled to herself.

Confused murmurs rolled through the crowd of the trio cartel members, as Katy pulled Delilah level above her head, crouching slightly as she did. The trio members looked confused. They all had automatic weapons in their hands, but it was like they didn't know how to use them, like their hands were seized. Finally, the lead member stepped forward and laughed, as he pulled his gun to level and squeezed the trigger. The shot was never fired though, as the weapon fell useless in front of him and his bleeding arm with it. He looked at the half of his arm still attached, as blood shot in streams like a raging fountain. Katy grinned, as she reveled in the man's screams, watching as the realization dawned on him and the rest of his gang what they were up against. It lasted for only a second, as Katy jumped, twirled, and brought Delilah onto the side of the man's neck, following through to the other side. His head rolled to a stop in the headlights of the SUV where the light glowed on his wild confused eyes. Great torrents of crimson liquid shot from his neck, as his headless body shook then fell forward onto the packed dirt floor beneath him.

The others pulled their guns to level and rushed toward her, maybe realizing their death was imminent if they did nothing. *Big mistake, but one she was happy they made, as Delilah was a thirsty girl after all. She needed all the blood from assholes she could get.*

Katy dispatched them quickly, as her thoughts faded away and she was one with her blade. Delilah opened a hole in her that could only be filled with death. Katy was the maestro and Delilah was the instrument of destruction, as she whirled through the air, nearly a blur and almost unseen to the naked eye.

Shots were fired, machine gun blasts echoed throughout the hangar, but the bullets went wild, never hitting their intended target. You couldn't focus on what you couldn't see. She pushed Delilah through the eye of one man and the blade jutted from the back side of his head for only a moment before it was pulled out. Delilah was buried into another before the man hit the floor. Katy cut low and sliced upward, leaving a huge hole in one trio member. He watched with shock, as his guts fell on the ground in front of him.

In the end, not one of the ten cartel members was left standing and their bodies lay strewn across the floor, piled in a river of blood, running in different directions. Body parts lay in scattered pieces and guts rolled out into the mess from the gaping holes left in their bodies. A coppery aroma mixed with the smell of feces permeated the air inside the hangar. She was so wrapped up in her fury, she forgot the rival cartel members were behind her, until she heard one of them retch and empty his dinner onto the floor. Katy smiled, as she stood ankle deep in the gore with Delilah covered in the blood of the trio men. They paid their debt to her. The one they made the minute they stepped forward.

She turned to her brother and noticed he was staring at her. "What the hell was that all about?" He looked to the middle of the hangar, staring at the scene in front of him, as disbelief dawned on his face at the eviscerated bodies lying on the floor. "The old man did teach you well. I had no idea you could do all that," he shook his head. "Where'd the scared little girl go to?"

Katy laughed and looked at her blade, "There's no fear where Delilah is concerned, only death," she pointed the tip of the blade in his direction, "She's the devil's concubine and don't you forget it."

She walked into the crowd of cartel members and then stopped in front of one of them. He marveled at the petite girl in front of him and the steadiness of her nerves, even with the blood and pieces of flesh stuck in her hair. She smiled at him, then reached for a handkerchief in his breast pocket. It was white and silky and the coolness of the fabric on her fingers eased the hot blood coursing through her. She brought it to the blade and wiped Delilah clean, then handed it back to him. She smiled, blowing him a kiss, and sheathed Delilah in the leather case.

Her reputation would only grow from there. No one in Mexico knew her as Katy. She was the Devil's Concubine and if Delilah was with her, she lived up to the hype, as the power to kill coursed through her when she held her magic blade.

Now, as she sat in the back of Lenny's car, Katy felt some of the old confidence come back while she cradled Delilah in her arms. It'd been torture behind the walls of the prison, but she was becoming whole again and ready to take her rightful place as Delilah's mistress.

The car drove through the city, down Decatur Street, then turned toward Bourbon. As they drove past the famous street, Katy could see the revelers were already in full swing. It was midday, but it didn't stop them. The party was getting started and would get wilder as the day carried into the night.

Lenny made his way slowly and methodically through the narrow streets, driving down Bourbon and the tourist sections near Jackson Square.

"Why are we taking the scenic route?" she asked.

"I thought you might want to see some of your old stomping grounds," Lenny mused. "Maybe you could check it out later. You know, once you get settled in."

Katy shrugged but didn't say anything, because she knew where they were going. They drove out of the old city and crossed the bridge until they were in the Algiers Point District. They exited onto a narrow city street and drove a few blocks. Katy saw the familiar home she grew up in ahead of them and the house was as unassuming as before. A nondescript brick home no different than any of the others around it with the French style all too familiar in New Orleans. Ornate metal railings adorned the upper floors, surrounding balconies with doors leading to the rooms behind the walls. You could see across the Mississippi River and get a bird's eye view of Jackson Square. The top of the buildings at least, as the main view was the levee. Three large white garage doors lay in prominent rows along the bottom floor of the building. One of them opened, and Lenny drove the Chrysler inside. The door slid to a close behind them, as Lenny put the car in park. Lou stepped out of the driver's side, yawned, stretched, then opened the back door for Katy.

She stepped onto the concrete floor, as Lou reached in beside her and retrieved her bag. She placed the strap attached to Delilah's case around her neck and adjusted the buckle until Delilah lay comfortably on Katy's back.

Katy stood there, checking out the inside of the garage, reveling in the place she hadn't seen for three years. The old wood beams lay exposed at the top of the room with pressed tin tiles adorning the ceiling in between. They were drab though and nothing like the ceilings adorning the upstairs rooms. Where the halls stretched the length of the building, ending in tall ornate windows and doors that led to the balconies.

She remembered the night and what it was like before she went to bed sitting on the balcony outside her bedroom, watching over the French Quarter while listening to the sternwheel boats honking their horns along the banks of the Mississippi River. She could see all of it from her vantage point. She also saw cruise ships going by. The gargantuan boats were a wonder to see, as they looked like floating buildings, staying impossibly upright as they towered above the levee. That was a life she'd never know. Not the way she was raised. It was no different than her longings to settle down with Bob and raise kids. Katy let those desires fade, as she made peace with the cards she was dealt a long time ago.

Lenny stepped around the car and walked up to Katy. "Is it as great as you remembered it? The city," he waved his arm around. "This place?"

Katy nodded. "It's good to be home." she yawned, "I'm ready to see my daddy now."

Lenny pursed his lips and scratched his neck. "Well, you see he's..." his words trailed off as he looked to the ceiling for the proper thing to say, "indisposed at the moment."

Katy gave him an incredulous look. "What do you mean, indisposed? Lenny, you told me he was sick, but doing well. You said he wanted to talk to me, so why can't I see him?"

Lenny put up a hand. "No, I didn't say you couldn't see him, and he does want to talk to you. We just have to prepare for the meeting." He smiled, "You know, I don't want to surprise him or anything, the man has no idea you got out today."

Katy shook her head. "I don't understand. Daddy should've known I was out of prison. He sent me letters all the time and I told him the exact day of my release date," she sighed. "What are you not telling me, Lenny?"

He let out a heavy breath. "It's like this. You know how the old man was always messing with that voodoo, hocus pocus shit?" Lenny shrugged, "Well it may have caught up with him," he put his hands up, "all I'm saying."

Katy looked away from him. It was more of Lenny's shit, and she was growing increasingly frustrated by it. She thought she may have to take matters into her own hands soon enough if he kept it up. Katy was no different than Lou, standing close, and waiting for further instructions. She turned her gaze back to Lenny. "So, you're telling me he was a victim of his own magic?"

Lenny pointed in the air at her, "Bingo. He shouldn't have been messing around with the dark arts anyway."

"You know, Delilah was created by the dark arts you speak of," Katy smirked. "Daddy told me so. I don't believe you, Lenny. Daddy wouldn't be that careless," she sighed. "I'm going to my room and getting a shower, then you're going to take me to him. Get it?" She said tapping against Delilah's handle, jutting out by her shoulder.

Lenny put his hands in front of him, "Okay, sounds fair, I don't want any trouble with the bitch." He leaned his head forward and tapped his foot nervously. "Tell you what. You get cleaned up like you said. Then you can see the old man," Lenny said. "But be warned, he ain't the same as you remember him."

Lenny turned to Lou and nodded. "Lou'll help you with your things up the stairs."

"I know the way," she protested.

Lenny smiled, then looked to Lou like he was no more than an object he controlled. "He needs the exercise."

The big man started for the stairs and Katy followed. She watched as Lenny made his way to the other side of the garage and toward the office where a group of people waited for him. They all stood as he entered and she watched curiously as all gathered around him like he was of great importance. Much like the way they did for her daddy. Katy had a bad feeling in her gut as she ascended the stairs behind Lou, up to the landing.

Lou sauntered along the long hallway leading to the main floor and opened the door at the end, motioning for her to step inside.

When Katy stepped into the main living area, she was filled with a sense of nostalgia. It'd been too long since she was last here and she looked around, taking it all in. The curtains hung from ceiling to floor, long and flowing, like white waterfalls disappearing into the hardwood boards below. Katy remembered hiding behind them as a child while Lenny frustratingly looked for her. She scanned the room and could almost remember the innocent little girl running through the hallways, hiding from her brother, or the various nannies her daddy hired to take care of them. She looked to the other end of the room and saw two large double doors with ornate fleur de lis carvings in the middle, standing majestically in place. Above them was a large statue of Christ hanging on the cross, looking down on those who passed. Katy smiled, remembering how the statue always seemed to be watching her, no matter which way she turned. Her daddy would touch his feet before entering the library, he said, for luck. His strange sense of religion and magic all blended into a convenient soup, paying little attention to what the Catholics or Protestants thought. He had his own way of creeping around the edges of what seemed normal to most people.

She looked back to the doors and smiled, knowing what was on the other side. It was her daddy's library. The room where he practiced his magic. She wondered for a moment if he was in there but dismissed the idea, as he was probably in bed upstairs.

Katy followed Lou down another hallway, leading to a staircase at the end. It led to the living quarters for the orphaned children her daddy took in. The workers for his operations. They slept right above the library and studied in a room on the other side of the hallway. She herself did the same when she wasn't being taught Martial Arts and sword fighting. The charges were home schooled here and also learned the business of what it meant to be adopted by Kenneth Bergeron.

Her bedroom was on the top floor, where it'd been since she was at least thirteen. The big man breathed heavily as he ascended another flight of stairs. Katy was sure at this point he was wishing for an elevator. She smiled wanly, remembering there were no working ones in this place. The old freight elevator had been broken down for years, as her daddy neglected to fix it, opting for the exercise of walking up and down the stairs. He was an impractical man, but cunning and tough at the same time.

Lou stopped at the top of the last staircase, caught his breath, then walked a few steps and sat Katy's bag by her door. He slowly made his way to an antique chair sitting in the middle of the hallway and sat in it. His large body caused the wood to creak in protest, as he leaned his back against it and let out a long sigh. "Damn, why don't they have any elevators in this place?" He took in another deep breath, "I'm gonna need a pack of smokes to get over this one."

Maybe smoking is your problem. Katy mused, but didn't want to get into the merits of Lou's health now, as she was too busy breathing in the smell of the place. It had an ancient quality you didn't get in the antiseptic halls of the prison. This place had a scent all its own, like a living breathing thing with a familiarity she cherished. She soaked it in, hoping she'd never leave it again.

Katy looked at Lou. "Thank you for the help, but I can take it from here."

He nodded then reached into his coat pocket, producing a pack of off brand cigarettes. He motioned with his head toward the stairs at the end of the hallway. The ones leading to the roof terrace. "If you don't mind, I'm going to head outside for a pick me up, before going back down." He stood with a grunt, as his knees cracked and he grimaced from the painful effort of standing. Lou limped a little before walking to the door leading to the staircase. Then he opened it, hesitated, sighed, and started for the roof. She heard the creak of wood, as he made his way up.

Katy thought it odd he would go up another flight of stairs to smoke but paid no attention to him, the man didn't look like he could think for himself very well anyway. She picked up her bag and turned to the door of her bedroom. The same fleur de lis pattern of wood carving found on the main floor adorned this one as well. It was much smaller, but the pattern was consistent throughout the house, as the entire place had the air of the old French Quarter, even if the real one was across the river from it. The entire New Orleans area was steeped in tradition and art, but there was also an underbelly of darkness only brought on at night, in the backrooms of jazz halls and bars. Many had secret areas only known to those connected or the unfortunate soul who accidentally wandered in. Some of those people vanished forever, seeking adventure, but getting more than they bargained for. New Orleans was full of mysticism and magic, and it bristled with excitement, rarely sleeping even when the tourists were in for the night. Katy knew of many of these places. Where she could meet with friends, close down the night, and maybe even finding the right man or woman to meet her needs if she so desired. She needed a good fuck. After she checked on Daddy, she would go out on the town. It'd been too long since she had any fun.

Katy opened the door and breathed in the air of the place, noticing her room was just as she left it. The porcelain clown dolls lying on chairs in each corner, kept their vigil, watching over the vacuous space. The punched tin ceiling tiles–common throughout the house–were especially prominent here. Katy knew each one by its distinct design, as she studied them at night before going to sleep. Each had a small moon in the center, the symbolism she didn't understand, but the vision was spectacular. A little present to help lull her off to sleep and give her sweet dreams. She sat her bag down on the bed, placing Delilah next to it, then lay on the bed and got comfortable. In a few minutes she was fast asleep.

When she woke the room was darker and dusk had descended on the horizon outside. She thought it strange she slept so long, but she supposed she was more tired than she realized and this bed was comfortable. Much more than the ones she had been used to for the past three years. Katy put her legs over the side of the bed, then stretched and yawned. She looked at the clock on the wall and saw it read seven o'clock. She considered it and realized she had slept for a long time.

Katy stood and made her way to the bathroom on the other side of the room and after she undressed, she stared at her naked body in the mirror for a moment. She looked the same, maybe a little tighter from losing weight. She was a solid one-twenty when she went in and figured she was around one-fifteen now. Her belly was flat, and she needed a shave in her nether region, as she was never one for too much hair there, opting for a clean shaven look. She didn't want her lover getting unwanted extras in their mouth when they went down on her.

She stretched her arms over her head, watching as her tattoo–a pattern of oriental letters–elongated with the pulling of her skin. It took up a length of her body from under her breast to past her hips. She had other tattoos as well, like the one on her forearm with the Spanish words for Delilah's nickname. She loved them all, as they were her calling cards. Some showed off and others were clear warnings of the danger ahead.

Katy turned the handle of the shower faucet as far up as it would go and let the stream heat up before entering, then stepped in and pulled the curtain. She breathed in the steam and relaxed. The thought of taking a shower for the first time in three years without someone standing guard had a nice appeal. The idea freed her mind, and she let the hot stream of water soak her until the stress of prison life, and the last three years was washed away.

The water turned lukewarm, and she turned it off, then stepped from the shower and toweled off. Katy wrapped the towel around her head, tucking her hair inside to dry, and walked naked into the bedroom. She stared at the chest of drawers across the room and wondered if her clothes were still there. She was sure they were, as Katy doubted Lenny graced the door of her room since she was gone, opting instead to have someone do it for him.

She pulled one of the drawers open and was happy to see all her clothes just as she had left them, folded in their proper place. Katy grabbed a pair of jeans and a loose fitting t-shirt, then opened the top drawer to retrieve a pair of panties and a bra. She put the bra on first and adjusted the straps until her breasts were tucked away, then slipped the panties on. She removed the towel from her head and let her hair fall over her shoulders and grabbed the shirt and pulled it over her head. She went to the bathroom to find a brush and brushed the remaining water from her hair and pulled it back into a ponytail.

Katy looked at herself in the mirror, placing her arm in front of her and stared at the words of her tattoo. *La concubina del diablo.* The words rang true. Katy returned to the bedroom and sat on the edge of the bed and gathered her boots. The thick soled black boots looked more combat than fashionable, but Katy liked them that way. *Better for shit kicking.* She thought.

She pulled her boots on and tucked her switchblade knife into her sock, then picked up Delilah, sliding her arm through the shoulder strap. She cinched it down tight and reached for the handle of the blade to see if it was easily accessible. She was ready. It was time to meet up with her daddy.

She walked across the room and grabbed the door handle. Katy turned the knob and eased the door open, stepping slowly into the hallway, and turned her head from side to side. There was no one there. Her nerves were on edge and deep in her gut she felt something was wrong. She moved quickly toward the stairway, stopping for a second at the top riser and looked down, seeing nothing but the dark room below. The were no lights on, as Katy descended the first set of steps, then stopped at the bottom to scan the area.

The house was eerily quiet, all except for the low muffle of a party from across the street. Katy stepped into the hallway of the second floor and walked across to a room on the opposite side. She opened the door and looked in the room. Beds were lined up against the walls and she heard the light snores of the children in there. She closed the door gently, so she didn't disturb the sleeping charges, but thought it strange how they were all asleep so early.

The hallway was darker now with only a sliver of outside light left, as the waning sun was disappearing behind the horizon. Katy made her way to the stairs leading to the main floor and started down them, holding her hand against the wall. The other resting on the handle of Delilah ready to strike if needed.

She made it to the bottom of the staircase and crouched by the newel post. Her fingers tapped nervously on Delilah's inlaid bone handle, as she eyed the room ahead of her. It was steeped in shadow with no lights on anywhere, like some cavernous hole deep in the earth you got sucked into and never seen again. She thought about trying to flip the light switch, but considered the shadows to be helpful, as she was trying to be stealthy anyway. The glow from the little bit of light outside was more than enough for her to see what she was doing.

Katy stepped away from the stairs and headed toward the large double doors of the library, walking under the watchful eye of Christ.

She reached up and touched his feet for good luck. She noticed him watching her with curiosity like she'd changed since the last time he saw her, maybe she had. She pulled Delilah from her sheath, then reached for the door handle with her free hand. She hesitated before opening the doors, instead leaning in and placing an ear on one of them to listen inside. She heard a light crackle, like the flickering of a flame and the smell of incense burning filled her nostrils. The same sagely smell her daddy burned when he was conjuring. It caused flooding waves of nostalgia in her brain and increased her desire to go inside.

She opened the door and whatever she expected to see in her daddy's room of magic had no bearing here. Her mind had to adjust to a different reality. Her daddy lay strapped to a large cross in the middle of the room, propped diagonally on a wooden support. His body was strapped to it at the wrists and ankles with large ropes, holding him securely in place. His arms had streams of dried blood streaked from the crease of his elbows down to his wrist, where it dripped into some kind of container for collection.

Candles burning in skull holders surrounded him and his body lay lifeless. A lump of flesh consumed by the dim light of the room. She saw another empty cross adjacent to him. Lenny stood cloaked on the other side, harkening to the image of some dark priest with arms stretched out in a welcoming gesture. As if to say, come one, come all, were all worthy of this feast before us. A table was in front of him with a large book opened on it, one she'd never seen before, as it was much larger than any of the one's her daddy used.

"Lenny," she cried out. "What is all this?"

He laughed. "Why, this is the sacrifice to the one and only, the last of your supper," he nodded to her daddy, "and the last of his."

Katy understood the reference he was making, but failed to see why he was doing it. She started for her daddy, paying no attention to the other in the room until it was too late. A woman stepped in front of her with a knife in her hand. She was dark skinned with long cornrow braids along her scalp, flowing onto her shoulders. She wore a white robe that was sheer enough to see her naked body through it. Her dark nipples protruded from under the cloth, causing the fabric to rise from her chest. Katy raised Delilah, but before she could swing, the woman blew a powder in her face. Katy wasn't prepared for the suddenness of the attack and breathed in the offending substance. Within seconds she felt woozy as the woman stared at her with large white eyes, floating in a pool of ebony skin. Katy saw two of her, as she felt herself falling. She landed with a thud on her bottom and the woman quickly crouched beside her, cradling her head. She heard the Caribbean accent of the woman talking softly to her. "Sleep my little dove, sleep."

Bad choice of words, Katy thought but could do nothing to protest. She felt herself being eased onto the floor in a supine position. The floor should be cold, hard, and uncaring, but to Katy it might as well have been a mattress, as she was floating on air.

The next few minutes were like an out of body experience, as Katy felt like she was being lifted into the air then dropped. Her arms and legs were heavy, but she could feel them being stretched and cinched down tight. She looked in front of her and saw her daddy there, tied to his cross, head slumped, and blood pooling into the collection container she saw earlier. She wanted to reach for him, caress his face and hold him, but her arms wouldn't obey. Her head was foggy, and she was finding it hard to concentrate.

Katy pulled at her restraints, but she was too weak to do anything, as a wave of nausea came over her and she vomited the contents—the little she had—onto her chest. The sour smell of the vomit, mixed with the incense, left a faintly putrescent odor in her nostrils. She concentrated on her daddy to see if he was alive but didn't see him. She saw Lenny. Katy blinked her eyes and tried to focus. She was mixing the image of Lenny and her daddy together in her hallucinatory state.

She heard Lenny talking to her. "Hey, girl, you coming around?"

She turned her head away from him, but toward him at the same time. This was so fucked up. "Lenny?" Katy said groggily, "the fuck are you doing?"

He laughed, then nodded to the woman beside him. The same one who blew the powder in her face, "Latoya," he said.

The woman sauntered toward Katy, carrying her knife. Katy saw Delilah hanging loosely from Latoya's shoulder and wanted so badly to reach for her. Latoya hovered a smaller knife above Katy's arm. With a surgeon's precision, she cut a slit from the crease of Katy's elbow to her wrist, causing blood to pour from her wrists into a collection chamber like the one below her daddy. Latoya repeated the procedure on the other arm.

Katy weakly raised her head and spoke. "Who the fuck are you anyway?"

Latoya looked her in the eye. Her thick Caribbean accent rolled off her tongue in an almost scolding fashion. "I'm Latoya Bordeaux. I enchanted this blade for the woman who first used her," then tilted her head in the direction of her daddy or Lenny, Katy wasn't sure, "and him," she patted Delilah. "You've been well suited to her, but now the circle must end."

"You're the Santería my daddy spoke of." Katy said in a near whisper, but what she said made no sense. Did she add the magic to the blade for Katy? "Why are you doing this to him?"

Latoya regarded the figure on the cross adjacent to Katy and shrugged. "Because he asked me to." She turned away and Katy tried to concentrate on what she was saying, but her head was in too much of a fog. Why would her daddy ask to be hung from the cross? It didn't make sense, but then, none of this did.

She heard Lenny chanting louder, as he looked at the book on the table and reading it as he conjured whatever evil he was perpetuating here. Latoya stepped beside him and began to sing as well. The smell of fresh incense wafted past Katy's nose, and she felt nausea come over her again, but she had no strength left in her body to convulse. She only dry heaved and coughed. Katy winced, as fire shot up from the floor and continued until it formed a circular barrier around the two crosses, leaving the rest of the room inaccessible. The ground beneath her was turning red, as pieces of the floor fell away into some pit below. The garage she thought should be there ceased to exist and the cross she was tied to teetered forward then fell back again, jarring her body from the sudden quick movement.

Katy craned her neck to the side and through the flames she saw her girl. Delilah was no longer on Latoya's shoulder but lying in a chair about ten feet away. Katy grimaced as she felt the heat of the flames. It caused her eyes to water, and she winced from the uncomfortable tears. The flames continued to rise until she couldn't see the room anymore. The incense was replaced by the smell of sulfur coming up from below. Through the watery mess of her vision, she saw more tiles break away. Through the crackle of the fire, she heard Lenny laughing then speaking commandingly to the pit of fire below. "Take them, take them! They are yours my king."

She watched the tiles crumble below her daddy's cross, as it teetered for a moment on the edge of what was left of the floor, then impossibly closer to the side. Katy stared at him, wanting to reach out and pull him away from the edge of the chasm. The heat and the blood loss were causing her to see things, as she looked at him, no longer seeing her daddy, but Lenny in front of her. The tiles were falling away at a rapid succession under him and his cross dropped, then teetered forward, righting itself for a moment. It was dangerously close to the edge of the ever-expanding pit below.

Katy coughed violently and the force of the reaction caused her cross to lean forward away from its holder and closer to the fire. She pushed her back into it and pulled against her restraints, struggling with all she had. The cross righted itself and fell back into place and she noticed her struggles caused one of the ropes to give a little. She could feel herself waning from consciousness, but she couldn't pass out. She wiggled her hand back and forth, pulling with the remaining strength she had and felt the ropes loosen a little more. Katy cried out as the heat intensified on the bottom of her feet. She made a vain attempt to pull away, as a few more tiles fell into the pit, and she could feel the cross teetering again. A roar came from below and she heard fresh laughter on the other side of the fire. It sounded like her brother, but as she stared at Lenny in front of her, she had to wonder what the hell was happening here.

The sulfurous smoke rising from the pit made her cough. Her head was pounding, as the heat intensified, but she wouldn't be deterred. The chamber of blood under her daddy, or Lenny, or whoever the fuck he was, fell into the pit below and the fire leapt in response, increasing in size. The cross on the other side of her teetered, then fell through the tile beneath it up to the midsection, as the fire lapped around his body. The rest of the tiles holding it in place gave way and the cross tumbled with its occupant into the pit below. Katy watched as a ball of fire consumed him, then he was gone. The sight of this caused her to renew her efforts to loosen her restraints. She pulled harder against the ropes at her wrist, feeling the sting of the abrasions on her skin. She sucked in, trying to ignore the pain, but her body was wracked with it along with the exhaustion she felt. Her hand was numb, and her arms were heavy. She felt her strength waning, but she wouldn't succumb to the weakness. She already had too many times. The Greta's and the Lenny's of this world had no hold on her. She was Katrina Sanchez, and when she held Delilah, she was so much more. Katy needed her thirsty girl and no matter what the barrier, she'd get to her.

Katy pulled with all the strength she had left. Her arms screamed at her, and it felt like they were being pulled from the socket, as she twisted and contorted to get free. She jerked and pulled, as the ropes dug at her wrists, making whelps and blistering her skin. The heat from the fire only added to the discomfort. She felt the rope loosen and she pulled again, feeling her hand come free. Her hand was free but it gave her little comfort, as she couldn't massage her wrists or soothe the pain in any way until she was completely free. She stretched for the blade in her sock, inching her fingers closer, trying to grasp it. The collection container with her blood in it fell forward, tumbling into the pit. More flames jumped from below, nearly burning Katy's hair, as she jerked her head away.

The violent movement caused the cross to ease forward. She felt it and pushed her back into it to keep it from toppling into the flames. Lenny, or whoever the fuck was on the other side of those flames, cried out louder. The pitch of his voice going up an octave. She looked down and saw the cross was suspended by one last floor tile. After this one, she'd have no chances left. She wiggled the other restraint, but it wasn't budging, and she had no strength left in her arms, so she pulled at her bound feet. They were crossed over one another, just as Christ was on the cross, only instead of being nailed, she was tied. A mistake on her captor's part. Katy breathed slowly, sucking in smoke and coughing, but she wouldn't be deterred. She wiggled her legs back and forth in a see saw pattern and felt it give a little. She jerked her legs, pushing down, then up, anyway she could get the ropes to loosen. Her head was woozy from smoke and blood loss. She felt fresh friction burns under her pants, but she pushed the discomfort away.

The cross jumped, but instead of falling forward, it fell downward, like an unstable pogo stick. Then she felt it teetering again, easing forward, and Katy pulled with everything she had. To free herself and right the cross. *One last pull.* She said to herself. *This is it.*

She jerked upward and the leg came free. The heat was unbearable, as the wall of flames nearly touched the ceiling. Even though she felt like she was cooking from the inside out, she was thankful the fire was hiding what she was doing. They probably figured she was already in the pit. The smell of burning rubber filled her nose, as she looked down and saw the bottom of her boots smoldering. Her head was swimming from the heat and exhaustion, but she didn't let it deter her. She raised her leg toward her free hand, trying to stifle her coughs for fear of being detected, as the flames were licking at her body. She needed fresh air, or she would die here.

Her fingers inched their way toward her sock. She felt the switch-blade and started moving it up and out. Katy winced when she touched the hot metal of the knife handle. She eased it out a little more, until the head of the knife was showing, then grasped it with her index and middle fingers, pulling it free the rest of the way. An inhuman scream bellowed below her, as fear gripped her insides as to the possibility of what was down there.

She flipped the knife into her hand, nearly dropping it as she did. The fuzziness in her head was clouding her judgement, like she was drunk or drugged. It didn't matter, she'd be feeling nothing but pain if she didn't get free.

Katy pushed the button on the blade and heard the familiar snick. She turned it toward the ropes on her other wrist and began to use it in a sawing fashion. The rope unraveled in seconds, and she pulled her hand free. The screaming below intensified, and she felt the cross start to sink. She pulled her other foot loose the rest of the way, then turned over with her stomach toward the face of the cross.

Another tile holding it fell into the fire, as the cross slid downward a little closer to the fire, then stopped. Katy climbed faster until there was nothing left to hold. Her foot found the top of the large wooden holder, and she used it to launch herself into the air, as the cross fell into the pit. Katy covered her face, as she tucked and rolled through the wall of fire, landing on the other side and tumbling to a stop on the cold floor. It felt refreshing for a moment, as she took a deep breath of fresh air. She rose to her hands and knees, noticing her shirt was on fire. She tucked and rolled, then quickly pulled the fabric over her head and threw it to the side, then rose to sitting. Her whole body was a sooty, smoky mess and blood dripped from her wrists. She took what was left of the smoldering shirt and quickly tied the fabric around her arms to stop the flow of blood. Small tendrils of smoke rose around her, but she didn't mind them, she was focused on one thing only. Delilah.

Lenny and Latoya were still conjuring on the other side of the flames and hadn't noticed she was free. She took advantage of this and ran toward Delilah, but was cut off by Latoya before she could get to her girl.

"Stop," Latoya screamed, waving her arms in front of Katy, "you are trespassing on sacred ground."

Katy looked at her like she had two heads. The nerve of this woman. "Last I checked, bitch, I live here and maybe it's you who don't belong."

A roar came from the pit and Latoya turned her head toward it. Katy used the temporary distraction to jump for Delilah, but Latoya saw her and jumped too. She tackled Katy in the middle and rolled her to the floor. Katy reached forward, her outstretched arms trying to find purchase on anything. She had to get to Delilah and slice this bitch into oblivion.

Latoya elbowed her to the side, then punched her in the ribs. The woman had sharp elbows and it felt like a knife punching into Katy. She winced but ignored it, as Katy had been hit harder. The beast in prison for one. She was determined to get to her girl.

A voice cried from beside the pit, not the thing below, but one she recognized as easily as she breathed. "Stop what you're doing, Cher. It's silly dat you fight like you do."

The women stopped and Katy stared at him. Her eyes wide with the recognition. "Daddy?" She said, staring in disbelief at the man in front of her.

He laughed. "In the flesh, well, maybe not mine, but dat's all in the eye of the beholder I suppose." He nodded to the fiery hole in front of him. "Once your no count, shit eating brother fell in the fire below, I reverted back to my original self, and here we are."

Katy shook her head. "I don't understand. You mean that was you and not Lenny in the car today?" Katy turned to consider the pit, "Lenny was on the cross?"

He clicked his tongue, then sighed. "Poor, boy," he drew a cross on his chest and looked to the ceiling, "God rest his soul." Then he looked at the floor, and rolled his eyes toward her. "Sorry, wrong god." He laughed, low and ominous. "Yeah, he was on there and good riddance to him. You know, he tried a hostile takeover of my operation? Who dat boy think he was dealing with?" He furrowed his brow in disgust, or maybe pain, it was hard to tell, but Katy could tell he was visibly uncomfortable. "I got no use for someone like dat. You on the other hand, I wanted to keep. But my hands were tied. The deal was for both of you. So, you wanted to talk, better make it quick," he turned his head and gestured toward the pit, then looked at her, "because what's coming from there, gonna be looking for you."

Kenneth Bergeron stopped talking and his face contorted, as he grimaced in pain. Something was writhing below the surface of his skin, as tendrils of dark veins snaked down his arms. Black boils rose and burst, spewing brackish liquid down onto the floor. Katy watched in horror, as the man she called daddy, changed into something inhuman. His laugh turned to anguished howls, as he raised his head and cried out.

Katy had to do something, or she'd become fodder for the monster coming from the pit. Latoya grabbed for Katy to renew her grip, but Katy slammed an elbow into the side of Latoya's head. The woman screamed, letting go and giving Katy the space she needed to retrieve her blade. She stood and brought Delilah over her head, then ran toward her daddy. She was stopped before she could get to him, knocked forward by Latoya and hitting the floor with her chin, arms splayed before her. Delilah rolled to the side and Katy started for her, but Latoya began pummeling her with clenched fists in the ribs. Katy tightened her stomach and rolled into Latoya. She wrapped her legs around the woman and pulled her into her body. Then quickly wrapped her arms around Latoya's, straightening them against her body so she couldn't swing them anymore. Katy pulled her head back and brought it down hard onto the bridge of the Santería priestess's nose. The woman may know her spells, but she didn't know how to fight. Katy released her and Latoya jumped to her feet, holding her bleeding nose. She groggily reached into a small pocket of her cloak and Katy watched Latoya bring it to her mouth.

Not this time, bitch. Katy thought. She dropped to one knee and swung Delilah low, slicing across both of Latoya's Achilles tendons. Latoya howled, as she fell forward to her knees and unclenched her fist, dropping the powder on the floor. She pushed herself to her hands and crawled away from Katy and toward Kenneth Bergeron, as blood poured from her injured foot, leaving a trail behind her. She reached out and touched his feet, then wrapped her hands around them, then looked up at him.

"Help me," she cried with desperate tears rolling from her eyes.

He laughed with a crackly, deeper voice. He crouched beside her and wrapped a hand around her arm and with one quick pull, he tossed her into the fire. Katy gasped, not at all expecting this and watched the look of confusion and surprise on Latoya's face, as she grabbed the air, then disappeared into the fire. The flames shot higher in response to the new sacrifice.

"Now, it's just me and you, Cher. The way it was always meant to be," he said. His sultry Cajun voice, the one Katy adored growing up, was gone. He had a deep hollow one now, a voice coming from some dark crevice. One that crawled from hell.

She looked at him; the red laughing demon who once was her daddy had answers and she was going to find them. "Why did you masquerade as Lenny and why go to all this trouble? What is it you want?"

"For one, Cher, I couldn't go to that prison, or any other for that matter," he said, a tinge of sympathy in his voice, one Katy thought derived falsely. "They'd have me in a second. You don't get to my level without making enemies, in the criminal and civilian world," he looked at the book on the table. A trail of thick smoke rose from it, leading to the fire wall around the pit, "Dis here was what got you there in the first place. Dis book taught me so much. With the help of Latoya," he nodded toward the fire, "the devil rest her soul, I was able to shape shift and call the one who's gonna give me power beyond my comprehension," he smirked. "Lenny came to me wanting to learn things. He wanted to be able to wield a blade the way you do, or anything to give him an edge. Like I said, he wanted my business, and didn't want to wait for something dat was never gonna be his to begin with." He smiled. "He was supposed to take the fall that day, not you. I allowed him too much freedom and lost my daughter in the process. I went to great lengths to change my appearance and take Lenny out of the organization," he shrugged. "To do so, I had to make some promises to certain deities." He looked at her with a semblance of pity in his glowing eyes. "My plan was always to have you by my side, my girl, the one I trained from your youth, but the one who comes, wouldn't let me."

Katy gave her daddy an incredulous look. Lenny was right when he came to talk to her in prison. He tried to warn her but she didn't listen. Now she had to contend with what her daddy had become and whatever was coming. "What do you mean the one who come?"

As if responding to her query, howls of torture rang from deep inside the pit. Katy's daddy turned toward it. He threw the robe off, seemingly irritated by the thing and Katy could see his body was a red as the fire shooting from the pit. He stood in nothing but a loin cloth, like ancient people would've worn. Katy was happy he was covered, because seeing her daddy naked was not a vision she wanted to visit. His belly hung over it, red and crawling inside, like little worms were trying to get out. He spoke in a voice older than him, like an ancient priest atop a pyramid, preparing for a sacrifice. "Talk to me oh ancient one. Come forth to make me whole." He cried out, as the flames rose, licking the ceiling, causing pieces of smoldering paint to fall on the floor.

Anger boiled in Katy, as she moved to avoid the debris. She wondered if the children above were okay. She didn't have time to wait for what was coming, this place was falling apart, and she had to get out of here. She'd check on the charges as soon as she did.

She turned for the door, but was stopped by a dog's paw, blocking her path. Katy looked at the pit and saw a large snout with impossibly huge teeth, snapping in the air. It snarled, as it tried to fight its way from the pit. It pushed until its head was showing. Then she saw two more snouts on either side of it, only their noses though. It was a three headed dog, but only the middle head and one paw could fit through the opening. Katy was sure it wouldn't be long until all the paws were up here. She backed away from the paw and turned to her daddy.

His head had grown. It was grotesque and oversized. Red with a longer chin and pronounced as he laughed louder. "It's working!"

Katy stared at him in disbelief. What kind of monster was he? "Daddy!" she cried out. "Stop this. What is that thing?"

He whirled to her. "It's 's da protector, Cher. Cerberus who watches the gates of hell. The creature has been let loose to prepare the way for the one to come."

Katy shook her head. "I don't understand. What's coming?"

He looked at her. His mischievous grin gave a grim recognition of what he knew already. "The devil, Katrina. He's coming to take his child home. I gave him one, but he didn't get the one he really wanted."

Katy pondered this. "Me? I'm the devil's child?"

He laughed. "Yes, girl, your momma was the true devil's concubine," he nodded at Delilah. "Her spirit is in that blade. Why do you think you wield it so well?"

She looked at him confused. Until now, she always thought she was adopted. Her mom nothing more than a piece of street trash and thrown to the wayside with all the rest of statistics. "I thought my momma died on the streets. A victim of drugs."

He shook his head. His Cajun accent wasn't as sweet and had a guttural quality. "Aw, Cher, not all things are to be taken as the truth. Maybe half truths or somethin'. This might be the case here," he clicked his tongue. "Your momma got around. We worked the dark magic together, but she saw an opportunity to gain the power of the great deceiver. She lay with the devil himself and became his lover, his concubine. Me and Latoya were able to bring her back, but with one caveat," he nodded toward the machete, "the result is your blade. Your momma, Delilah, is trapped in there. Why you think you wield her so good?"

Katy looked at her blade, admiring her even more. It all made sense now. Delilah was an extension of her because they both flowed with the same spirit, one Katy felt every time she held the blade. It was why she was such a mess in prison. Without Delilah, Katy wasn't her whole self. They were like two halves and only powerful when together.

Cerberus roared and the vibrations sent shivers through Katy. She pulled Delilah to ready. Her daddy smiled as he watched the creature advance. "It's alright, my girl, don't be afraid. The devil will have his due," he said. "If you'd have fallen in the pit, this would all be over. But you had to go on and make it difficult. He's gonna come up here and get you himself."

The protector of hell's gates clawed at the floor, trying to gain purchase. He slid backward a bit, then pulled himself to where he was a moment before. He looked at Katy, sniffed the air, then lifted his head and howled, like a large hound dog baying at the moon. The enormous canine lay its head on the floor and winced. Small pimples of fire rose from his spine. Cerberus shook his body like a dog would after its bath. Blobs of fire fell onto the floor around the large dog. The fire blackened to char, then began to slough off. Gray colored demons emerged from the ashen shell. They had short legs and long arms with hands touching the floor. The creatures leaned into them the way an ape would. Their faces were slack with cheeks drooping over their mouths, like a bulldog. They gathered, snarling, and frothing at the mouth, as they all turned, staring at Katy.

She looked at her daddy. He was laughing, seeming to enjoy the show.

Katy turned to him. "What do you have to gain by doing this?" She asked him, "why don't you just let me go? I thought I was your favorite?"

He grinned, "Dat's true, child, you were my project. You learned quickly and have an untamable spirit in you," he said, looking at her apologetically, "but all good things come to an end. When the devil found out he had children he didn't know about, well, I suppose a trade was in order."

Anger boiling in her, as she produced a scowl of distaste on her face. "You sold your children to the devil? What did you get in return?"

"Why, everything I ever wanted my dear child. You and your brother's sacrifice will give me power beyond anyone in this world could ever imagine. Once this is done, I'll be more than mortal, I'll be a demi-god. Unbeholden to any authority on this planet. I'll probably start by running for president. I dare any opponent to get in my way."

He has lost his fucking mind. Katy thought. She had to end this. She looked beyond him and saw the book was continuing to emit smoke around the fire ring. It was sending incense into the air. She could smell it, mixed with the sulfur odor, making a primordial smoke ring around it. The pit seemed to be dependent on the book keeping it open.

Katy felt a sting on her wrist, as one of the demons grabbed her. She saw smoke coming from the area of her skin it held. She tried to pull away, but it was too strong, it didn't matter, because the hand she held Delilah in was free. She swung Delilah around, bringing her onto the shoulder of the demon. The blade sliced all the way through, separating the demon's arm from its body. An inhuman fury of anguished cries came from it and the rest of the demons and the hell dog whimpered as well.

Katy grabbed Delilah by the handle with both hands and swung her like they were up to bat in the ninth with the bases loaded. The blade found its target, splitting the demon's torso into two pieces. It had a look of surprise, as it fell to the floor in front of Katy. She watched in horror, as eyeless worm like things crawled from inside its detached body. They writhed on the floor with rows of sharp teeth snapping in the air. They looked like parasites or some kind of intestinal worm being detached from its host. Katy brought her heavy boot down on one of them. It screeched as gray ooze shot from both sides of the thing. She stepped on another, before the rest scurried away toward the pit.

Katy smiled and raised her blade to level in front of her. "Delilah has spoken. Which one of you bitches want the rest of her?"

The demons looked at each other. They all had puzzled stares, like they weren't sure what she was saying.

"Do your masters bidding, you inept pieces of shit," her daddy called out.

Katy reset herself, as two demons came running toward her. She felt the power of her blade surge through her body. It's slice and dice time and she and Delilah were charged and ready. The devil had come to Louisiana and Delilah was the golden fiddle.

Katy ran toward the rushing demons, as they reached for her. She avoided their grab, jumping over them instead, bringing Delilah into the middle of one of demons' misshapen heads. Horrifying screams filled the room from the anguished pain of another fallen comrade. Katy heard nothing, as she was in slaying mode. She dropped to her feet behind the decimated demon, then pushed Delilah through the middle of the other. She pulled the blade upward, slicing through the top of the creature. Both fell to the ground as useless lumps, as the worms crawled at her feet. She squished a few more for good measure, then turned for the other demons.

Three down, seven to go. Katy watched as the rest of the demons surrounded her daddy in some vain attempt at protection. She moved her head to the side, hearing a crack in her neck. She looked at them and smiled. "Bring it on, motherfuckers!"

They didn't advance though, only stood their ground. They weren't getting out of this so easily. She ran straight toward them, swinging Delilah over her head in a circular motion. Just before she got to demons, she dropped to the floor, letting her momentum slide her forward, slicing Delilah through the ankles of one of the demons. It fell forward, its large arms extended to try and break its fall. The little worms fell from it and attached to Katy's boot. She shook them off, but one went flying, landing on her stomach. It bit down on her exposed skin and Katy felt it trying to burrow into her stomach. She smacked at it but before she could stop its advance, the pile of demons fell on her.

A tenuous moment went by, then a howl rang through the demon hoard and Cerberus cried in anguish. Delilah emerged from the top of the pile. Intestinal worms crawled on her handle, screaming in confused protest. The blade rotated, carving a hole for Katy to escape. She jumped through, spinning and twisting through the air, throwing the intestinal worms in every direction. Some hit the wall with a wet scrunch, then slid down, leaving a trail like some slug sizzling in a salt bath.

The demons that were left scrambled, trying to reform the circle, but Katy wasn't deterred. She sliced Delilah through the outside demon closest to her. It fell to the side, as the worms left its body and headed for the pit. Katy scrunched some under her foot. She felt something move inside her when she did. It was the worm that crawled inside her stomach. She could feel it trying to attach to her. It seemed to be distraught over its fallen comrades, because each time she stepped on one, it squirmed furiously.

There were three demons left and instead of circling her daddy, they all came for her.

"Stop her. She's just a girl," her daddy cried out. Funny, Katy thought, how he looked at her with weakness all of a sudden. He trained her, so he should know that she was fully capable to take care of anything against her.

She spun in a circle, using the centrifugal force to bring Delilah through the middle of the first two demons with one blow. Katy fell to one knee after the effort, holding a hand in front of her for balance. Katy's head was tilted forward and she slowly brought it up to face the last demon. It stood in front of her daddy, who was already picking up the book and moving toward the other side of the room. She could hear Cerberus howling behind her, clawing at the floor, trying to break free of his bounds. The floor shook beneath her, rising and falling with each anguished movement of the gargantuan dog.

The demon in front of her was bigger than the rest. She thought it strange as they were all the same size when they first fell off Cerberus. She didn't care, she'd take this one down just like she did the rest. It raised its hands and to Katy's surprise, blasted molten fire from its balled fists. She jumped, dodging one blast, the other hit Delilah as Katy raised her for protection.

She felt the heat from the attack and realized if she made one wrong move, she'd be done. She had to find the inner beast only Delilah could give her and become the essence of the devil's concubine. To release the power of the chains around Delilah and become less slave and more the master.

Katy concentrated and jumped into the air, spinning in a circle. She felt her body rise farther, until she was suspended over the demon. She didn't know why she was hovering the way she was, but she reveled in it, feeling Delilah's power surge through her.

The demon directed its blast toward her, but as it hit the blur of activity she'd become, the molten fire shot harmlessly to the side. It hit the walls instead, bursting them into flames. The drapes caught fire, as the old fabric was consumed, like it'd been hit with a shot of gasoline.

Katy continued to spin for a moment more, then stopped and dropped down on the demon so fast she was nearly undetectable. She brought Delilah in a large arc on the demon's arms with the force of the swing cutting cleanly through its outstretched appendages. Katy landed on her feet with her arms extended and the end of the blade stuck in the wood from the force of her swing. The demon continued to shoot projectiles from its arms, but instead of fire, it was now blasting intestinal worms. The things came straight for Katy, screeching inhuman wails, as they snapped the air.

She heard a loud scream come from the pit and it sounded anguished and hurt. Cerberus barked along with the screaming, then looked at Katy and growled.

Katy paid no attention but pulled Delilah from the floor instead, just in time to intercept the first of the worms. Her blade deflected the thing into the air and its gelatinous middle burst in a gush, as it tumbled into the fire from the pit. Katy jumped and twirled, her body extended in an arc, as she somersaulted her way toward the demon.

The worms hit her boots and legs, as well as Delilah. She felt the one inside of her moving frantically each time one of its brethren met their demise. She kept going until she was in front of the large demon. It never stopped shooting the slimy projectiles, like it was in a trance unable to discern for itself what to do. Katy jumped high in front of the gray slack jawed demon. The launch gave her the momentum she needed to come down on top of the demon, allowing Delilah to split the monster from head to crotch with one quick blow.

Katy landed on her feet, crouched and ready for the next assault. It never came. She looked at the demon. It stood there with a confused look on its face, as its eyes turned inward in a strange, crossed fashion, then it separated, each part of its body falling harmlessly to the side. Katy stood and scanned the room for her daddy and saw he was near the entrance to the room. The book was still producing a smoke trail that flowed onto the floor, keeping the portal open. She wondered how much longer he'd use the book to keep the portal open? What would happen when the thing coming from below got here? She had to get to him before they found out.

"I'm coming for you old man," she called out.

He held the book in his arms, looking at her with his face a crumpled mess of disdain. "You think you've won this, but the devil will not be denied his prize. He's coming for you, Katrina."

She heard the cries from the pit, as the room shook. Cerberus had two paws and one of its three heads completely out of the pit now. The other two heads had their snouts and eyes showing, as they all sniffed the air. Their large mouths drooling and panting. The pit was growing. It would be the size of the entire room soon, as long as the book continued producing smoke.

She started to run toward her daddy but was stopped by one of Cerberus's large paws. It crashed in front of her; the heat of its skin causing the floor to char. She saw the other coming, swinging in the air to bat her around like a ball. She rolled onto the floor toward the wall to avoid it and the large dog started chasing her, like she was a play toy it needed to grasp in its paws. The dog snapped the air and smacked its large paws, as Katy dodged and parried to avoid it.

She brought Delilah into the smoldering flesh of the dog. Cerberus howled, as he swung the other paw wildly. Katy jumped again, but not fast enough, as the large pad of his foot caught her and sent her reeling through the air and hitting the wall hard. She was momentarily dazed and Cerberus took advantage of the situation, as he homed in on her, pouncing in Katy's direction. He wasn't completely out of the pit but had enough reach to hit her.

Katy saw it coming but didn't have time to avoid the attack. She extended Delilah in front of her and the blade sliced through the webbed part of the dog's paw. Cerberus yelped, pulling his paw away. Katy jumped to her feet. Her eyes widened, as she saw all three heads of Cerberus extended from the pit now. She noticed something else. Around each of the necks of the massive beast, there were fiery chains, pulled taught, extending into the pit. The chains looked like large dog leashes, connected to the neck of Cerberus. *Who was holding them on the other end?* She wondered.

Cerberus stopped paying attention to Katy and began to pull at the floor with his large paws, trying to gain purchase. The realization dawned quickly on Katy that whatever was coming from the pit, the dog was helping it climb up.

Katy looked at her daddy. He held his hands up over his head and she saw his eyes glowing as he stared at the pit. "Come oh bringer of death, the lion who roams the earth in search of destruction," his Cajun accent deep and craggy with a sing song quality, making it more ominous. "Oh, you've been gone for too long, come forth and bring your power, your glory to me!" he called out, laughing with delight.

Katy looked at the pit in horror, as she saw Cerberus's body was out of the pit. The large hell dog's three heads hit the ceiling, but the chains extended into the pit, keeping him at bay. All three heads howled and barked, making a thunderous sound and causing the whole house to shake with renewed fury. Flames shot high from the pit, hitting the ceiling, causing it to burst into an explosion of flames. She thought about the children in the rooms above them, and wondered how much more the house could take before it fell around them all. She also wondered if the children were still up there. She backed against the wall, keeping Delilah extended in front of her, as she stared in surprised terror at what was coming from within the pit. A large hand reached for the sky, then slapped the ground. Fire sizzled on its reddened skin. Black veiny protrusions rose like small mountains on its arm, snaking in different directions. They were scaly like slick black snakes writhing along the arm to the hand. A roar, like some great lion echoed throughout the room, causing Katy to shake with fear.

Her daddy was distracted, using the book to keep the pit open for the beast within. She snapped out of her stupor and calmed her nerves. Now was her chance, there wouldn't be another. Katy brought Delilah over her head, spinning her furiously around in a circle, running to get to him before he looked up. She jumped into the air a few feet from where he stood and spun, floating forward like a ballerina performing the finale to the dance, as effortlessly as breathing. With her momentum, she brought the blade down, not on him, but the book. A large crack sounded as the ancient paper exploded, not cutting it, but closing it instead. The smoke ring dissipated and faded away, as the book fell from her daddy's arms and hit the floor. He stepped back, shaking his head like he'd come to his senses. He stared at her. "What have you done?"

She looked into his eyes. They were wide, but not looking at her. He was focused on the pit. Katy turned toward it. Two arms were on the ground now, and she could see a head popping out. The pit had extended outward, nearly touching the wall on the other side of the room and leaving only a few feet in front of Katy and her daddy. Cerberus stood on the side of the opening, barely able to keep his massive frame from falling back into the pit.

A shiver ran through her as she saw the thing in the pit. Its hideous head protruded from the hole in the floor. Two horns jutted from the top of its head, curving upward, and extending out to the side. Two more horns jutted from behind its pointed ears and curve downward toward its shoulders, nearly touching the area. They were black as the deepest night. Tendrils of smoke rose from the horns and Katy felt a rush of fear go through her, as two large elliptical striped, yellow eyes stared back, focusing on her. It wasn't fully out of the pit, but she could see enough to know she didn't want to see anymore.

She turned to her daddy. "What is that?"

He looked at her with disgust, as anger rose in his voice at the transgression she'd perpetrated on him. "It's the destroyer come to take us from this world. The devil himself. I had control, but you just took it away from me when you closed the book. It won't open again unless you say the right words. If that book doesn't go back to hell, then the devil can run free as long as he wants," he threw his hands in the air, "I ain't sticking around to see who he favors. It's on you now," he turned for the door, grasping the handle, then turned back to Katy. "I got to go, Cher. May God help you."

Katy noticed his skin wasn't red and pulsing anymore. He was reverting to his regular paunchy old man form. She reached for him, grabbing his wrist, and turning him around, "the fuck you are!" Katy yelled in protest.

She spun her daddy in a circle, letting go, and hurling him toward the middle of the room. He rolled head over foot, resting near where Cerberus was sitting. He got to his hands and knees and shook his head, then screamed as he turned to see the hell hound bringing his large paw onto his head. She heard an audible crunch of bone, as blood spewed from both sides of the dog's paw. Cerberus's heads came down next, grabbing and fighting over the meaty morsels left over. They snapped the air, then licked at their paws to lap up the remaining blood.

Katy stared in disbelief, looking at Cerberus, then the devil as he emerged from the pit. His whole head was showing. He grinned and she could see sharp pointed incisors hanging from the sides of his mouth. A forked tongue slithered forward, like a snake fishing the air for its prey.

Katy saw the book lying in front of her. She gathered it up just as a sharp pain hit her stomach, doubling her over. She fell to her knees and dropped the book at her feet. Something was biting her inside and she knew what. The worm that burrowed in was trying to keep her from completing her mission. It bit her again, much harder and she punched her stomach, looking up at the devil. He smiled, then she watched as he turned his fingers into a fist. The worm burned inside her, moving and biting, and then releasing, only to get another hold.

She heard a laughing in her mind, as a man's voice spoke to her. One of authority. "You are my body and my blood, I give this all to you," he said.

She heard screaming from within the hollowness of it. Anguish and gnashing of teeth, like a thousand people spoke at once every time he said something in her mind. The worm bit her again and Katy felt as though her insides were being turned into hamburger. She spit blood onto the floor, feeling woozy, as the heat in the room threatened to overtake her. If she didn't move soon, she'd succumb to it.

"Why do you fight my child? Come with me and rule the world, we'll take it all. Watch," the devil said to her. He didn't move his lips, because this all came from within her mind. A sudden blast of brilliance flooded her vision and she saw herself on top of a large building. The world beneath her was on fire. She held Delilah high in one hand, and a severed head in the other. She recognized the face. It was a world leader, maybe the president or someone else, but the message was clear. Then she turned to see the people below her, as they were enslaved and being beaten by the same gray demons she defeated. One of the people looked up at her. It was a young girl who reminded Katy of herself only a few short years ago. The anguish in the girl's face made Katy feel compassion for her. She knew all too well what it was like to be controlled, put away, and forgotten by those above you; never allowed to have your say. The image of the girl emboldened Katy. Fuck the devil. She shook her head, and she was back in the room. She coughed from the smoke and spit fresh blood, as the worm bit down again.

Katy cried out, as the devil laughed inside her head. The same as before with painful crying in the background. She ignored it, fighting against the pain, as she picked up Delilah and stuck the point of the blade in the floor in front of her. Katy reached for the book again, gathering it in her arms, as the worm bit down again. The pain was excruciating, as a fire burned in the pit of her stomach. She felt like she wanted to vomit and thought maybe it would be the best way to rid herself of the offending creature inside of her. But she had a feeling it wasn't going to let go until she dispatched its master and sent this book back where it came from.

Katy stood on shaky legs with the book hugged against her. The devil screamed inside her head. He wasn't fully out of the pit yet but was fighting furiously to break free. She heard him bark commands to Cerberus and the large dog stepped in front of her. All heads were growling, as the great dog was ready to pounce. Katy stood her ground, but she didn't plan on going through the dog. She mustered the last remaining strength she had and threw the book into the air. Katy watched as Cerberus stared at the book with a peculiar fascination. The ancient book tumbled upward to nearly his line of sight. His head rose, watching the book, as it fell back toward the ground. Before it hit, Katy, with both hands on Delilah swung the blade like a bat. She hit the book, sending it toward the pit.

Cerberus grabbed for it, but it was moving too fast and whizzed by him, hitting the devil on the chest. The book bounced from him and fell into the fire below.

A howl filled the air, as ominous and dark as any Katy had ever heard, like a wolf crying lonely in the night with anguish too deep to fathom. She covered her ears, as the room shook violently and pieces of ceiling fell on her. She covered her head, but it was nothing more than a few pieces of plaster and some of the tin ceiling. Katy looked up to see the room above the library. To her amazement no bodies were falling, no one was up there at all. She was lucky to avoid the worst of the debris, she may not be next time. She had to get out of here before she ended up buried in the burning building.

The devil pulled at the chain around his dog's neck. He was trying to fight the force pulling him back down below and he screamed, grabbing for purchase, but couldn't stop his descent. Fire shot from below, like a geyser from a long extinct volcano. Molten slag puked from the hole, covering the devil, as his head disappeared. Katy watched as his hands and arms grasped the air and pain shot through her midsection, doubling her over again. Cerberus whined and scratched at the floor but found himself following his master into the pit, as the room was now engulfed in flames. They crept up the ceiling and Katy felt the heat taking her over and she had to get out of this room before she was cooked from the inside out. She tucked Delilah into her sheath, then covered her mouth and made her way to the door. She grabbed the handle to open the door, feeling the heat sear her hands. She pushed the door open and tumbled into the living room, falling to her hands and knees. Katy felt a wave of nausea overtaking her and she vomited blood onto the floor and chunks of meat came with it. Katy noticed something squirming in the blood pool and vomiting. She could see it was the worm. She pulled Delilah from the sheath and brought her down onto the worm and it screamed as it was cut in two.

Katy felt heat permeating her body from all sides. The fire was rolling over the ceiling above her, as smoke filled the room, and she couldn't breathe. Her lungs were burning as she inhaled the noxious fumes. She stumbled for the opening to the stairway leading to the garage. It was engulfed in flames, and she couldn't access it. She looked around the room in a desperate attempt to find an opening. She saw the large door toward the front of the house but saw the fire had consumed them. The windows and the drapes adjacent to the doors were still intact though. Her legs threatened to give up on her, but she trudged forward and pulled down one of the drapes. Katy wrapped herself in it and took a couple of steps backward. She stumbled forward and crashed into the glass. The flames, sucked forward by the fresh air, propelled her onto the balcony, rising in the air above her. She felt the balcony shift forward, threatening to fall away from the house. She picked herself up, keeping the drapery around her body to protect her from the flames, then jumped to the street below. She landed on her feet, but just before they made an impact with the pavement below, she instinctively rolled forward to lessen the brunt of the fall. Katy felt a sting of pain go through her shoulder. She also felt glass shards digging into her back, along with the sheath Delilah was nestled in. It took her breath, and she breathed out a whoosh of air, coming to a stop on her back, the drapery covering her face. She breathed in the fresh air, thankful for the feeling of it and coughed a ragged breath.

She saw light coming from somewhere, even though it was dark outside. The drape was removed from her face suddenly, and she saw a woman standing there in a fire suit and hat, scanning her eyes with a flashlight.

"You okay lady?" She said, as she crouched beside her with a medical kit.

Katy looked at her name tag. It said Kathy. Funny, it was almost her name. Kathy was a very pretty lady with blonde hair flowing over her shoulders and green eyes that seemed to draw Katy in. She wanted to ask her out but was a little too dazed at the moment. Katy moved and winced from the pain of her aching body.

"Sit still," she put a hand on Katy's shoulder, making her grimace. "We have a unit on the way," Kathy said. "I'm the paramedic who'll taking care of you."

The paramedic opened her kit, then began doing an assessment on Katy's busted body. Katy could feel the possibility of broken bones somewhere inside. She had other injuries she was sure she wasn't aware of, as she spoke weakly, "the kids. Did they get out okay?"

Kathy smiled at her. "Yes, the large gentleman over there," she nodded to her side, "I think his name is Lou. He helped them all to safety. If not for him, they would've all perished. He's a hero."

Katy turned her head to the side and saw Lou standing next to the charges and smiled. Guess she underestimated the big lug after all. She lay back and watched as Kathy pulled a needle from her case. "This'll help with the pain," she said, tapping the side of it. She brought Katy's arm toward her and pushed the needle into the crease of her elbow. She deposited the contents into her arm and Katy felt warm liquid fill her veins. "There you go, all better."

Katy smiled at her, feeling the effects of the medication overtaking her senses. She felt Delilah at her back and wanted to make sure she'd be there when she woke up. Katy looked at Kathy with foggy eyes, "My blade on my back, make sure it stays with me."

Kathy looked at her strangely, then noticed the handle of Delilah sticking from its sheath on Katy's back. "Yeah, I think we'll have to take it off when you go to the hospital, but I'll personally make sure it gets back to you."

Katy smiled, as the world around her faded away.

***

Katy's stay in the hospital was wrought with strange dreams. She fell in and out of consciousness a few times and would wake to the sight of the red faced demon her daddy had become. It disturbed her and she screamed out. The nurses made sure she had something to soothe her. One night in particular she woke to the sound of howling. The room was dark, but she heard something, not in the real world, but from the farthest reaches of her mind. The sound turned to a sort of whining, coming from the shadows. She rose to sitting in her bed and saw a red wolf standing in the doorway. Its eyes glowed yellow and had elliptical centers. It showed its teeth, not growling, but smiling, she thought. It howled again, then vanished into the darkness. She was only visited once by it but got the message. If she thought her real father was done with her, she better rethink that scenario.

Kathy did as she said and kept Delilah in a safe place in the storage room of the hospital and even left a personalized message attached to Delilah's sheath for Katy.

Left for you in good faith. Hope you find yourself in good shape. From one survivor to another. Love, Kathy.

Katy wasn't exactly sure what she meant by the survivor part, but she meant to find out as soon as possible.

Now, she stood outside the burned shell of her daddy's old building. She was all alone, having lost her brother and daddy, but she was determined to move on. Her daddy's estate was left to her, as there was no one else to take it. He'd mentioned her to his lawyer—another shyster, but at least on her side—and the man had no problem signing what was left of her daddy's money over to Katy. It was a pretty penny, even with the expenses given to the city for cleanup.

Lou stayed with her and even visited her at the hospital, bringing a few of the charges with him. The ones the city hadn't claimed yet. He figured most of them would end up in the foster system, except for the few over eighteen. Lou was a good guy and seemed to have a heart of gold. His change of boss may be a better fit for him. Katy hoped so anyway.

Katy was ready to move on. All that happened seemed to push her destiny forward. She had big plans for the business, even changing it up a bit. The criminal enterprises she was once involved in—mainly the drug trade—had lost their shine. She thought about branching out and since money wasn't a problem, maybe she could help others instead of hurting people all the time.

She pushed those thoughts away for the moment, as she sifted through the ashes of the area, she believed to be her father's library.

The city had done nothing to the burned out sight, only put caution tape around the perimeter. It was a welcome thing to Katy as it gave her an opportunity to look the place over before it was bulldozed forever. She sifted through ash, even moving a few boards, the ones she could, and found the one thing she thought may still be here. It was the book her daddy used to open the pit to hell. It was only a tool to give access, and not meant to be used any other way. Who knows what other things it could do. She planned to research it thoroughly and find out for herself. For now, it would be placed somewhere for safe keeping.

She'd have to secure a new place though. Katy had a lot to think about, but for now, she was going to find Kathy and see what she was up to. She patted Delilah's handle. "It's just you and me now, my thirsty girl. The power is within us."

The End

Afterword

Stories start as ideas. Small and sometime irrelevant; filed away in the back of an author's mind and occasionally brought to life if they scratch and claw their way out. This book was one of those ideas. It came from my desire to write something capable of instilling fear. A few years ago, I was sitting at my daughter's house out in the country, beyond the city limits. A place with enough forest around it to give the sense of being alone, like you were on your own desolate island with no one to call if trouble arose. I was headed to my car after visiting one night and heard her bloodhound howling his lonely call of warning, as he watched diligently over the property. Then I heard coyotes across the creek, yipping their response. It all gave me a sense this could be something chill producing. Add a storm, and a few other details, and you have the making of every B-rate horror film worth its salt. The one where the slasher is in the woods, just beyond sight, ready to strike at any moment.

A few months later and Within was born. It was meant to be a short story sent to a few publications, but as the original story was much too long for most publications who usually require the word count be in the 2000 to 5000 range—the original file came in close to 8500 words with revisions—and I felt if I cut anymore, the story wouldn't be true to my first vision. So, I held onto it for a while, as I worked on revisions to my novel Tent Revival. The novel was proving to be more difficult to finish than I first realized, and I felt there was going to be too much of a gap between my short story collection, Blues, Blood, and Love, and the novel. So, I decided maybe I should do a little project in between. My publisher at the time offered to give me the cover art for free, so why not publish Within as a short story in ebook only format? It was the first time I'd ever done something where there would be no printed version, so I wasn't sure how well it would go. I was pleasantly surprised. The slasher in the woods story garnered some great reviews by some respected authors and reviewers, and a reader who still says it disturbed her to this day.

Not bad, for something I figured would be sent to an anthology and never seen again until maybe I got the rights back. Once the story began to wane in popularity, I had to decide what I'd do with it. Send it out to an anthology that took reprints, or maybe use it as a reader magnet for newsletter submission. Either one of those options would've been viable, but as I reread the original short story, I knew it could be better. All it took was another idea I was working on, one of those scratching back there to get out. It was a very similar concept to the original Within, only with a sweet little twist, and I thought it would marry well with a few revisions to the original story. I'll let you decide if that's the case, granted you were able to read the original version before it was taken down.

I wanted this one to be a complete book though, with a print version and eventually an audiobook. I had another story I thought needed more. It had been rejected by a couple of anthologies and I soon found out why, restricted word count. Hurt needed to expand. To become more than a small, short story. To be subjected to a bigger, more open universe where I could explore possibilities without being told I had to put my story in a small box. By the time I had Within and Hurt together, I noticed a theme was emerging. One I couldn't deny.

Both stories were about broken women who faced situations out of their control and had to decide which way to overcome or succumb to the extenuating circumstances presented to them. After putting them together, I thought it needed one more story to round out the whole book. I was looking at a book with two stories that wouldn't even bring it to novelette size. I wanted something around the novella to short novel word count size. So, in comes The Devil's Concubine. I wanted it to be in line with the theme of the book, so it had to be a female protagonist. I started with one idea, a girl looking out a prison window into a visitor's room. It expanded from there into the longest story in the book and one I'm sure will spawn others. I'm thinking of a series of books even. Any of these stories could be turned into other books. They all have that potential.

Once they were all on the pages, staring back at me, I saw one major flaw. I was writing three stories about women, but from a male perspective. To make it authentic, I had to remedy this. I found just the solution I was looking for in a friend of mine and fellow reading junkie. Her name is Amber Applegate, and not only was she a beta reader and instrumental in helping this book find the right voice, but she also edited the whole thing. She's a fantastic beta reader and I used her on my novel, Soul Mirror, currently bouncing around out there, looking for a publisher. Now that I know she has editing skills, and is wanting to expand on that business, we will be working on other projects as well in the coming years.

This book has been a learning experience for me. I thought I knew about the ins and outs of self publishing a novel, but I found out, you never stop learning. Thank you so much for reading and spending your valuable time with me inside these pages.

Edmund Stone, May 2023

Also by the Author

The Rebecca Mythos series
Tent Revival
The One
Lost Hope

The Within Series
Within: A Three Part Horror
Punish: The Sequel to Hurt
Delilah: The Sequel to The Devil's Concubine

Chapbooks
The Gift of the Shadows

Short story collections
Hush my Little Baby
Blues, Blood, and Love

Books with other authors
The Little Runaway

About the Author

Edmund Stone is a writer of horror and suspense, and a part time boat captain. He resides in a home along the Ohio River with his wife, four dogs, and a group of mischievous cats. He is the author of six books and two short story collections. He has several short stories residing in various anthologies as well. His books can be found on Amazon and a few independent sellers.

Find him at edmundstonehorror.com or at https://linktr.ee/edmundstoneauthor

Edmund Stone Horror

Contact him at riverrevivalpress@gmail.com

While on edmundstonehorror.com, be sure to sign up for my newsletter to get a free story and all the latest information on new releases from Edmund Stone Author.

Trigger Warnings

In an effort to avoid spoilers for readers who don't wish to see trigger warnings, I've included them here.

This book has one scene of animal harm in the first story and a scene of sexual abuse in the last. While these scenes could produce uncomfortable feelings for some, they do add to the dread and evil the protagonists must overcome. I never add gratuitous sex or violence to my stories for the sake of being there. It must relate to something within the story or it doesn't happen. I urge you not to judge the writing of this book on anything else than your entertainment and to enjoy a good scare. As a fellow horror reader, I'm always looking for the same.

www.ingramcontent.com/pod-product-compliance
Lightning Source LLC
Chambersburg PA
CBHW050346160726
48002CB00001B/483